What peo

Resetting Our Future: Feeding Each Other

The global food system is sick, and almost everyone knows it. But this bold, big-hearted book doesn't stop at diagnosing the problem—though it does that incisively and with style. Ultimately, *Feeding Each Other* offers something all too rare: It shows how we might heal. Auerbach and Civita's message hits with the force of a manifesto and the restorative power of an embrace. If a just, more joyous future is possible, it begins with the ideas in this book.

Joe Fassler, food and environmental journalist and author of *Light the Dark*

Auerbach and Civita reveal a food system rigged to fail our bodies, our communities and our planet. Driven by extractive profit and dismissive of love, life and human connectivity, this system can't last. It won't last, they help us grasp, unless and until we ground our food in a deeper understanding of power, rights and relationships. Reading this great little book will reconnect you to food and communities of the future in ways you didn't expect and help you understand and ultimately confront the toxic forces of unregulated agricapitalism.

Paul O'Brien, Executive Director, Amnesty International USA, and author of *Power Switch: How We Can Reverse Extreme Inequality*

All things move towards their end, so "sustainability" is ultimately an impossibility. It's a relief to read a rare book that stays with the trouble of collapse, of wisely navigating abrupt, fundamental change, and of building radically new sequels to our food systems. This is a guidebook for a new paradigm.

Shaun Chamberlin, activist, educator, and co-author of *Surviving the Future: Culture, Carnival and Capital in the Aftermath of the Market Economy*

Michelle and Nicole write authoritatively and passionately about our need to become more in tune with nature to transform not just our food systems but our lives. Food "predates money, markets, and media," they write, as they urge us to create more intimate connections with nature to find wholeness and joy within ourselves and our world. As a naturalist, and a lover of plant-based locally grown food, their message resonates deeply with me.

Melanie Choukas-Bradley, author of *Resilience: Connecting with Nature in a Time of Crisis* and *Finding Solace at Theodore Roosevelt Island*

Auerbach and Civita have done something quite special. *Feeding Each Other* begins with a deeply probing explanation of a highly complex and technical subject – the origins and untold impact of the food system on which all of us depend for sustenance. They then offer detailed, practical descriptions of the steps required for transformation to something sustainable and rewarding individually and globally. Anyone interested in a better future must read it; I guarantee you will be inspired.

Alan S. Miller, co-author of *Cut Super Climate Pollutants Now!*

Resetting Our Future: Feeding Each Other

Shaping Change in Food Systems through Relationship

Previous books

Resilience: The Life Saving Skill of Story
ISBN 1789047013

Resetting Our Future: Feeding Each Other

Shaping Change in Food Systems through Relationship

By Nicole Civita and
Michelle Auerbach

CHANGEMAKERS
BOOKS

Winchester, UK
Washington, USA

JOHN HUNT PUBLISHING

First published by Changemakers Books, 2023
Changemakers Books is an imprint of John Hunt Publishing Ltd., No. 3 East Street,
Alresford, Hampshire SO24 9EE, UK
office@jhpbooks.com
www.johnhuntpublishing.com
www.changemakers-books.com

For distributor details and how to order please visit the 'Ordering' section on our website.

Text copyright: Nicole Civita and Michelle Auerbach 2022

ISBN: 978 1 80341 488 1
978 1 80341 489 8 (ebook)
Library of Congress Control Number: 2023930910

A CIP catalogue record for this book is available from the British Library.

Design: Lapiz Digital Services

UK: Printed and bound by CPI Group (UK) Ltd, Croydon, CR0 4YY
Printed in North America by CPI GPS partners

We operate a distinctive and ethical publishing philosophy in
all areas of our business, from our global network of authors to
production and worldwide distribution.

The *Resetting Our Future* Series
At this critical moment of history, with a pandemic raging, we have the rare opportunity for a Great Reset – to choose a different future. This series provides a platform for pragmatic thought leaders to share their vision for change based on their deep expertise. For communities and nations struggling to cope with the crisis, these books will provide a burst of hope and energy to help us take the first difficult steps towards a better future.

—Tim Ward, publisher, Changemakers Books

What If Solving the Climate Crisis Is Simple?
Tom Bowman, President of Bowman Change, Inc., and writing-team lead for the U.S. ACE National Strategic Planning Framework

Zero Waste Living, the 80/20 Way
The Busy Person's Guide to a Lighter Footprint
Stephanie Miller, Founder of Zero Waste in DC, and former Director, IFC Climate Business Department

A Chicken Can't Lay a Duck Egg
How COVID-19 Can Solve the Climate Crisis
Graeme Maxton, (former Secretary-General of the Club of Rome), and Bernice Maxton-Lee (former Director, Jane Goodall Institute)

A Global Playbook for the Next Pandemic
Anne Kabagambe, former World Bank Executive Director

Power Switch
How We Can Reverse Extreme Inequality
Paul O'Brien, Executive Director, Amnesty International USA

Impact ED
How Community College Entrepreneurship Creates Equity and Prosperity
Rebecca Corbin (President & CEO, National Association of Community College Entrepreneurship), Andrew Gold and Mary Beth Kerly (both business faculty, Hillsborough Community College)

Empowering Climate Action in the United States
Tom Bowman (President of Bowman Change, Inc.) and Deb Morrison (Learning Scientist, University of Washington)

Learning from Tomorrow
Using Strategic Foresight to Prepare for the Next Big Disruption
Bart Édes, former North American Representative, Asian Development Bank

Cut Super Climate Pollutants, Now!
The Ozone Treaty's Urgent Lessons for Speeding Up Climate Action
Alan Miller (former World Bank representative for global climate negotiations), Durwood Zaelke (President and founder, the Institute for Governance & Sustainable Development) and Stephen O. Andersen (former Director of Strategic Climate Projects at the Environmental Protection Agency)

Resetting Our Future: Long Haul COVID: A Survivor's Guide
Transform Your Pain & Find Your Way Forward
Dr. Joseph J. Trunzo (Professor of Psychology and Department Chair at Bryant University), and Julie Luongo (author of *The Hard Way*)

SMART Futures for a Flourishing World
A Paradigm Shift for Achieving Global Sustainability
Dr. Claire Nelson, Chief Visionary Officer and Lead Futurist, The Futures Forum

Rebalance
How Women Lead, Parent, Partner and Thrive
Monica Brand, Lisa Neuberger & Wendy Teleki

Provocateurs not Philanthropists: Turning Good Intentions into Global Impact
Maiden R. Manzanal-Frank, President and CEO, GlobalStakes Consulting

Feeding Each Other: Shaping Change in Food Systems
Nicole Civita (Vice President of Strategic Initiatives at Sterling College, Ethics Transformation in Food Systems) and Michelle Auerbach (Educator and founder of Modaka Communications)

Unquenchable Thirst
How Water Rules the World and How Humans Rule Water
Luke Wilson and Alexandra Campbell-Ferrari (Co-Founders of the Center for Water Security and Cooperation)

Why American Baby Boomers Are Uniquely Responsible for the Climate Crisis — and What to Do About It.
Lawrence Schick MacDonald, former Vice President of Communications, World Resources Institute

www.ResettingOurFuture.com

Dedication/Epigraph

Perhaps the World Ends Here
 — Joy Harjo

The world begins at a kitchen table. No matter what, we must eat to live.

The gifts of earth are brought and prepared, set on the table. So it has been since creation, and it will go on.

We chase chickens or dogs away from it. Babies teethe at the corners. They scrape their knees under it.

It is here that children are given instructions on what it means to be human. We make men at it, we make women.

At this table we gossip, recall enemies and the ghosts of lovers.

Our dreams drink coffee with us as they put their arms around our children. They laugh with us at our poor falling-down selves and as we put ourselves back together once again at the table.

This table has been a house in the rain, an umbrella in the sun.

Wars have begun and ended at this table. It is a place to hide in the shadow of terror. A place to celebrate the terrible victory.

We have given birth on this table, and have prepared our parents for burial here.

At this table we sing with joy, with sorrow. We pray of suffering and remorse. We give thanks.

Perhaps the world will end at the kitchen table, while we are laughing and crying, eating of the last sweet bite.

Contents

Foreword

by Thomas Lovejoy

The pandemic has changed our world. Lives have been lost. Livelihoods as well. Far too many face urgent problems of health and economic security, but almost all of us are reinventing our lives in one way or another. Meeting the immediate needs of the less fortunate is obviously a priority, and a big one. But beyond those compassionate imperatives, there is also tremendous opportunity for what some people are calling a "Great Reset." This series of books, Resetting Our Future, is designed to provide pragmatic visionary ideas and stimulate a fundamental rethink of the future of humanity, nature and the economy.

I find myself thinking about my parents, who had lived through the Second World War and the Great Depression, and am still impressed by the sense of frugality they had attained. When packages arrived in the mail, my father would save the paper and string; he did it so systematically I don't recall our ever having to buy string. Our diets were more careful: whether it could be afforded or not, beef was restricted to once a week. When aluminum foil – the great boon to the kitchen – appeared, we used and washed it repeatedly until it fell apart. Bottles, whether Coca-Cola or milk, were recycled.

Waste was consciously avoided. My childhood task was to put out the trash; what goes out of my backdoor today is an unnecessary multiple of that. At least some of it now goes to recycling but a lot more should surely be possible.

There was also a widespread sense of service to a larger community. Military service was required of all. But there was also the Civilian Conservation Corps, which had provided jobs and repaired the ecological destruction that had generated the Dust Bowl. The Kennedy administration introduced the Peace

Corps and the President's phrase "Ask not what your country can do for you but what you can do for your country" still resonates in our minds.

There had been antecedents, but in the 1970s there was a global awakening about a growing environmental crisis. In 1972, The United Nations held its first conference on the environment at Stockholm. Most of the modern US institutions and laws about environment were established under moderate Republican administrations (Nixon and Ford). Environment was seen not just as appealing to "greenies" but also as a thoughtful conservative's issue. The largest meeting of Heads of State in history, the Earth Summit, took place in Rio de Janeiro in 1992 and three international conventions – climate change, biodiversity (on which I was consulted) and desertification – came into existence.

But three things changed. First, there now are three times as many people alive today as when I was born and each new person deserves a minimum quality of life. Second, the sense of frugality was succeeded by a growing appetite for affluence and an overall attitude of entitlement. And third, conservative political advisors found advantage in demonizing the environment as comity vanished from the political dialogue.

Insufficient progress has brought humanity and the environment to a crisis state. The CO2 level in the atmosphere at 415 ppm (parts per million) is way beyond a non-disruptive level around 350 ppm. (The pre-industrial level was 280 ppm.)

Human impacts on nature and biodiversity are not just confined to climate change. Those impacts will not produce just a long slide of continuous degradation. The pandemic is a direct result of intrusion upon, and destruction of, nature as well as wild-animal trade and markets. The scientific body of the UN Convention on Biological Diversity warned in 2020 that we could lose a million species unless there are major changes in human interactions with nature.

We still can turn those situations around. Ecosystem restoration at scale could pull carbon back out of the atmosphere for a soft landing at 1.5 degrees of warming (at 350 ppm), hand in hand with a rapid halt in production and use of fossil fuels. The Amazon tipping point where its hydrological cycle would fail to provide enough rain to maintain the forest in southern and eastern Amazonia can be solved with major reforestation. The oceans' biology is struggling with increasing acidity, warming and ubiquitous pollution with plastics: addressing climate change can lower the first two and efforts to remove plastics from our waste stream can improve the latter.

Indisputably, we need a major reset in our economies, what we produce, and what we consume. We exist on an amazing living planet, with a biological profusion that can provide humanity a cornucopia of benefits – and more that science has yet to reveal – and all of it is automatically recyclable because nature is very good at that. Scientists have determined that we can, in fact, feed all the people on the planet, and the couple billion more who may come, by a combination of selective improvements of productivity, eliminating food waste and altering our diets (which our doctors have been advising us to do anyway).

The Resetting Our Future series is intended to help people think about various ways of economic and social rebuilding that will support humanity for the long term. There is no single way to do this and there is plenty of room for creativity in the process, but nature with its capacity for recovery and for recycling can provide us with much inspiration, including ways beyond our current ability to imagine.

Ecosystems do recover from shocks, but the bigger the shock, the more complicated recovery can be. At the end of the Cretaceous period (66 million years ago) a gigantic meteor slammed into the Caribbean near the Yucatan and threw up so much dust and debris into the atmosphere that much of biodiversity perished. It was *sayonara* for the dinosaurs; their only surviving close relatives were precursors to modern day birds. It certainly was not a good time for life on Earth.

The clear lesson of the pandemic is that it makes no sense to generate a global crisis and then hope for a miracle. We are lucky to have the pandemic help us reset our relation to the Living Planet as a whole. We already have building blocks like the United Nations Sustainable Development Goals and various environmental conventions to help us think through more effective goals and targets. The imperative is to rebuild with humility and imagination, while always conscious of the health of the living planet on which we have the joy and privilege to exist.

Dr. Thomas E. Lovejoy is Professor of Environmental Science and Policy at George Mason University and a Senior Fellow at the United Nations Foundation. A world-renowned conservation biologist, Dr. Lovejoy introduced the term "biological diversity" to the scientific community.

Acknowledgements

A book on relational change is clearly going to have a lot of people whose relationships and care spun the web for this project and for us as people. First of all we are grateful to our team of reader-researchers – hunters and gatherers of data and story who questioned us at every turn and made this book what it is: Mackenzie Faber, Heidi Myers, and Elias Berbari.

We are grateful to Tim Ward, who is insightful, incisive, and always right. And to Changemakers Press and John Hunt Publishing for taking on this book and supporting the change.

We have always loved Rosanna Morris because of her art and also her ethos. We are deeply honored that her work graces the front cover of this book.

The folks we interviewed who shared their ideas and passions with us so that this book could be filled with stories not our own: Josh Crane, Mara Jane King, Kelly Whitaker, and Isabel Foxen Duke. Some of the interviews from which we drew stories and insights came from the Thurman Conversations project so thank you to Allan Cole for creating and sustaining that project and to Elizabeth DeRuff, Nina Ichikawa, Sue Salinger, and Reginald Hubbard. Also, some of the interviews came from Michelle's previous book research with Selassie Atadika and Becky O'Brien.

The EcoGather core team of Nissa Coit, Nakasi Fortune, and Conner Ferguson, plus prior contributors Dakota LaCroix and Andrew Cochran, along with the amazing people around the world who work at each of our EcoGather partner organizations, those who lead course development and the many practitioners who shared their stories in interviews and case studies, helped us create a rich ground in which these ideas grew. Lori Collins-Hall and Christina Goodwin, as well, who helped hold the space for writing and editing, when all else tried to take it.

At Project Protect Food Systems Workers our colleagues and siblings in struggle: Fatuma Emmad, Damien Thompson, JaSon Auguste, Hunter Knapp, and Kassandra Neiss of Frontline Farming and Project Protect Food System Workers, Devon Pena, Founder and President at The Acequia Institute and anthropology professor, Caitlin Matthews the Food Systems Coordinator for the Tri-County Health Department, Jenifer Rodriguez, the Managing Attorney of the Migrant Farm Worker Division (MFWD) of Colorado Legal Services, Alexia Brunet Marks, an Associate Professor of Law at the University of Colorado Law School, Margaret Brugger Executive Director of Commún.

All of you who have studied with us as we moved through paradigms and who had the intellectual curiosity to follow us into unknown places. In particular, Emma Enoch and Dakota Rudloff-Eastman, who stuck around long enough to shift paradigms with us and are now living in the relational.

Our thinking has been additionally shaped by our collaborations, conversations, and friendships with Susan Schneider, Anne Barnhill, Favor Ellis, Laura Spence, Leah Bayens, Sarah Shulman, Myra Kornfield, Nicole and A.J. Carillo, Clementine Morrigan and Amanda Scott.

Our ancestors have been with us, supporting us and teaching us to understand the power of food and care: Joseph Civita, Jr., Joseph Civita, Sr., Rose Malette Civita, Angelo Lamarco, and Gordon Friendman. In turn, we cherish the opportunity to be good ancestors to our children – Matteo and Rowan; Zach, Emma, Zoe, Ben, Chris, and Sam, who feed our spirits, renew our perspectives, and inspire us to care our way through collapse.

Douglas Hallam fed us as we wrote. Allan Cole walked the poodles. Both of them have gone all-in on loving relationship with us, which makes everything possible.

And finally, we are both grateful and relieved to have written a book together. After a bill, innumerable courses, papers, consulting projects, articles, late night conversations, and life, this book is our intellectual and relational friendship bracelet.

Introduction

When it came time to edit this book, Michelle flew to Vermont so that we could write face-to-face. We hadn't seen each other in over a year, so when Michelle texted her arrival time, Nicole offered, with disproportionate zeal, "I'll pick you up at the airport, and we'll actually go out to eat!"

The quirky vegetarian restaurant Nicole was most excited about was full. No reservations, no wait list. No problem, though. The next place we tried told us, at 7:15, that they would not be seating any other customers that evening. We popped into the ramen place next door and learned that they were already out of chicken, eggs, and all noodles, which meant a 55-minute wait for bowls of broth and green onions. We, along with a growing group of other aspiring diners, continued roving downtown Burlington in search of sustenance and service.

We all encountered similar circumstances at the next three restaurants – full dining areas and apologetic hosts. We tried a dim sum place, a farm-to-taco restaurant, and even an upscale French bistro. No luck. We called a Chinese restaurant, who said they might be able to take us in about two hours... maybe. So we gave up and drove away from the downtown area and its tourist traffic. With at least an hour before the last seating, the waitresses at a wood-fired pizza place were wiping tables and dimming lights – they'd run out of dough and were closing up early. At that point, we realized we were inhabiting a useful metaphor. While all the news told us that inflation was out of control and people were too broke to eat out, all the restaurants were full. While there was talk of workers not wanting to work, all the restaurants were capably staffed. We were not seeing what the news was telling us we should see: understaffed, empty restaurants. And yet, hours were ticking by and we still could not find somewhere to feed us.

Finally, at the twelfth restaurant, we were warmly welcomed. Over a bougie version of bar food – vegetarian gravy fries and a kale Caesar salad – we tried to put the metaphor into words. There we were with time, money, a car, smartphones, search engines, and the desire to put our money into the food system. But we simply could not. There were no restrictions, no budgetary issues, no significant constraints and we could not, for hours, get access to food. We were not trying to navigate notoriously brutal and bureaucratic systems like SNAP benefits nor were we, this particular evening, trying to feed a family on a budget. We simply ran into a section of a food system, in a financially well-to-do section of a mostly White and upper middle-class town, that was not working.

It was not, in fact, a metaphor, we decided. It was foreshadowing. Right now, the most vulnerable people around the world face food system failure daily. Our comical Saturday evening quest for dinner and diversion is, of course, nothing like experiencing real hunger, malnourishment, or insecurity about where your next meal will come from. But it was a reminder of the trajectory all humans are on because some of us have, in recent centuries, been wedded to a fundamentally flawed identity predicated upon supremacy and dominance. For so many reasons, which we will explore in this book, the experience of seeking – and not finding – something suitable to eat could easily be the future for all of us, regardless of socioeconomic status, race, location, or privilege. As science fiction writer and futurist William Gibson said, "The future is already here – it's just not evenly distributed."

To fully understand the intersecting set of highly complex systems and driving forces that set us up for and accelerate this collapse, about which we speak at great length in Chapter Three, could take several lifetimes. If nothing changes, we can all just wait a few years and see what the end-stages of relying upon extraction and pollution, a growth-obsessed economic order, land consolidation, hyper-specialization, globalized supply chains, and disregard of planetary boundaries will serve up. We will have learned – the very hard way – why it is, in fact, important to know where our food comes from, how to coax it from the Earth, and how to share it in ways that create real abundance. And, we will have done it to ourselves. Or, more precisely, some of us will have done it to all of us.

Something happened when we went from being humans engaged in a continual quest for nutriment to being consumers in the check-out line. We, the folks who can afford to do so, stopped sticking our hands in the soil and scattering seeds. We stopped living with livestock and instead allowed the stocking of thousands of lives inside of tightly packed barns. We let farming become something done by curious combinations of plant geneticists and underpaid, overburdened workers (who happen to be as skilled as they are scorned). Our diets became the domain of crop scientists and commodities brokers. The art of food preservation became the conglomerated business of food processing. And in these transitions, a whole lot of harm happened.

The global food system is massive, influential, interconnected and complex. It has elements we don't always see, interconnections that are not obvious to the casual observer, and a purpose ironically contrary to what we assume it is. Some assert that complex systems require equally technical and complex interventions. We disagree. When it comes to something as fundamental as food, voluntary simplification and intentional reorganization seem to be in order. We need to be looking at the culture and the system, not just the data.

Both Michelle and Nicole write, think, teach, research, and engage in activism around food and farms. Together and separately, we have studied and received degrees in food systems, taught food systems at the college and graduate levels, created food systems and ecological education programs, written and passed a bill to protect food systems workers, been food systems workers ourselves, written about activism and change, studied trauma, written innumerable papers about food systems, and become experts in our fields. And yet, the book we wanted and needed, that would give guidance and hope for our future never showed up in all the research and study we did. So, we wrote it.

We genuinely love food and the people who work and care with food. We cherish the intimate connections created when we share food. Because both of us have worked in the food system as laborers, academics, educators, policy makers, and activists, we know there's no shortage of recipes for improving the food system. However, in writing this book, we're bringing a dish unlike others on offer. We propose that humans can and should center their efforts to nourish themselves on love, on care, on connection. We see these qualities as essential and entwined with the notion of sustenance. In other words, we seek relational approaches to food system change and take relationship seriously as an organizing principle.

We have the pleasure of knowing and being moved by many individual change-makers who come to their work in the food system motivated by radical, active love and committed to sustaining reciprocal relationships with people, the land, and food. But, we also know that too many of the legacy institutions and power brokers in the food system have other priorities. So we know that it could all be better. Not just a little better, but systemically and holistically better for all people, this rare and beautiful planet, and the other-than-human kin with whom we share it. If we build bridges where there is brokenness, we just may be able to heal centuries-old harms. If we start using the food system as a channel for love, which is itself the stuff from which meaningful life is nourished, we might not only find a way to keep things alive, but we might also experience resonance and joy in the everyday. Doesn't that sound so much more delicious than a future of scarcity and privation?

We focus on food not just because we need it, love it, and have studied it, but because food connects within, between, and through the social, environmental, and economic systems in which we live. It is an interaction with the life of the planet, and, arguably, the most intimate exchange between living beings and the environment. Food systems are, in essence, significant ways in which humans organize their continuances as hyperkeystone species in ecosystems. We interact with the environment in many ways – all too often with negative impacts. By focusing on food – something at once ordinary and sublime – we make visible the connections that sustain life and give it meaning. By focusing on the connections revealed through food, we can recognize the destructive nonsense of organizing our pursuit of food around nutrition over nourishment, of production over process, of profit over people and planet, and of systems of oppression over liberation.

Our thesis is simple: you can change the food system when you change the culture of it and relationships that make it up. We will take you through our solution in Chapter One. In Chapter Two, we will survey of the food system itself. Chapter Three will take us deeper into the potential crises that we are facing down (or ignoring). Chapter Four contains hope and direction in the form of the principles we suggest will change the system. Finally, Chapter Five delivers stories from places, organizations, and people who have already changed the world around them and the food systems in which they live, leaving you with living, breathing examples of how these principles work in the world .

A note on our point of view. We are writing in the United States. As a result, some of our arguments – especially when we can only illustrate with a single example – may come off as more U.S.-centric than they actually are. We draw from what we know and encourage readers to connect ideas we offer to their contexts.

In recent years, folks have started to recognize the limitations of linear thinking. It has become fashionable to see, study, and act upon systems. And so, people now analyze "the food system" in an attempt to get our arms and heads around this global behemoth that is at once almost everywhere and exceptionally unobtrusive.

For many of us (too many of us?), food is understood to be available so long as cash is available. Thanks to a highly productive "global food system," we don't have to think much about food and we can instead direct our attention to other things. Or, if we do think about food, we have the luxury to be entertained by it: to cloak chefs in celebrity, let our phones eat first, watch reality TV shows about cooking, or page through high production value cookbooks we never intend to open in the kitchen.

Here's the thing, though: food predates money, markets, and media. Despite massive global efforts to grind foodways into submission, something about the co-constitutive relationship between people, place, and food resists pure commodification. By co-constitutive we mean that people, place, and food make each other and form each other and not just that they have some passing or superficial relationship to each other. Food is, and should, be treated as special not only because it is essential, but also because it is part of the interconnected web of life and of love. As forces, love and life are a pretty potent combination. As educator, philosopher and change shaper bell hooks said in her book *All About Love*, "Love is an act of will, both an intention and an action."

We happen to take love seriously as force – one as muscular as it is mystical. But if, for you, it feels like a four-letter word best left unsaid in serious discourse, give us a chance to legitimize love and demonstrate why it is particularly potent and powerful when paired with food. For some extended time after our birth, humans (like all of our mammalian relatives) cannot feed ourselves. Prior to the industrial era, babies were fed in the most intimate way, from the bodies of their mothers (or caring surrogates). Because of some beautiful biological ballet, breastfeeding releases loads of oxytocin – the very hormone that calls up the swirl of emotions we call love. Beyond simply being an existential necessity, first food is first love. While the same endocrine mechanisms may not be in play when expressed milk or formula are fed, the closeness and caring connections create the very same conditions for love. These experiences prime us to associate food and care, love and survival. Later in our lives, food takes on different forms and is offered in different relationships – the bowl of pastina with butter, parmesan, and parsley your father makes when you are under the weather, the peanut butter toast that your husband feeds you when your child has finally fallen asleep in your arms. These, too, are made of love. The associations hold and food is capable of drawing and keeping us together.

In the eyes of economists, food becomes commodities to quantify and analyze, for historians a way to trace changes over time, for activists a sphere in which to intervene and create change, for legislators a way to keep peace, make sure their constituents are served, and gird the legitimacy of the state, and for city planners a way to improve the functioning and attractiveness of their locality. All of these views and many more, from biologists to doctors to parents to chefs, are all essential to move the food system forward and to prepare us for what is to come. We believe that no idea lives alone, and that ideas, banded together, can change culture and hence the world. So food can simultaneously be a subject of analysis and an expression of love. We invite you to let our ideas infuse yours, whatever your point of view. We want to bridge whatever separates us and we believe food has the power to do just that.

Chapter 1

A Deceptively Simple Recipe

We are part of a system that has been rigged to fail us. It has been rigged to fail our bodies and our communities and our planet while extracting profit from all three. So, when we talk about food systems change, the recipe is simple. Our first job is to say no to the status quo: Nope. No thank you. And this book will tell you how to do so. Then, we need to make changes to the system where we have the most impact. The change itself is a readily available ingredient: Relationship. For us, relationship is an active practice of nurturing connection and reciprocity. This is an especially powerful move when it displaces transactional behavior. Focusing on connections, and their quality, makes it easy to put our collective survival first, over our individual needs, fears, and self-interest. Relationship will also help us undo the damage caused by centuries of objectification and division caused by racism, colonialism, capitalism, patriarchy and all the other "isms." As we let our relationships go deep and spread wide, we experience a sense of belonging and meaning among kin.

In right relationship, we weave a web of caring connections in place of the current tangle of profligate extraction and profit – a snare we're all caught in by virtue of our reliance on the global food system. We will stare straight at the problems with how humans meet their food needs in the next chapter. Here, we want to offer the possibilities for change and the instructions for moving forward. Mucking around in all the problems of the food system can wait until we have laid out a path to the future and we can view the mess with new eyes. At that point, we will pick through the past for parts from which we can build the future.

We won't be able to offer the kind of all-at-once, sweeping change that turns over the apple cart and suddenly results in a just, sovereign, and ecologically balanced food system. What we are going to do is something much more realistic: save our lives and our communities using eclectic wisdom, some ingenious tactics, and the power of connection.

The path we will travel together starts with defining systems. We will then explore the most impactful ways to shift systems. From there, we bring you along into the new paradigm of what we are calling an "agrelational" food system. We will give you a tour of the problems we are now seeing in the food system and how they are likely to play out in the future. With the problem in mind, turn to a set of principles that will ground the work of all who wish to move toward an agrelational system from wherever we are. We are not writing a prescription for what exactly to do, because everyone's place in the system is very different. What we are doing is introducing the principles by which you can assess choices, impacts, policies, projects, and ways of life. Finally, because theory needs stories, we will give you an entire chapter of hope filled with emergent examples of people, places, ideas, and changes that have already happened so that you know how realistic this set of principles really is for the folks already making change.

Food Comes from ... Systems

The first thing to come to terms with is that the food system is a system. Thinking in systems is a skill. Changing systems is a bit like preparing a multi-course meal and getting all the food ready at the same time. Mental juggling is involved.

Donella Meadows brought systems thinking out of MIT and to the masses. She defines a system as "an interconnected set of elements that is coherently organized in a way that achieves something."[1] A system must consist of three types of things: "elements, interconnections and a function or purpose," all of which affect each other. In a system, not only do all the parts affect each other, but together those parts "produce an effect that is different from the effect of each part on its own." Systems exist from the cellular level to the universal level, and everywhere in between. Still, not every collection of things is a system. Some things are just conglomerations, tossed together without any particular connection or function. The pile of laundry on your floor, for example; that's just a heap. Toss another pair of pants on top and it's just a slightly bigger pile of laundry. Systems, by contrast, have an integrity and wholeness – and a set of active connections and processes that self-organize, repair, and keep them together.

Nicole picked up Donella Meadows' small but paradigm-shifting book *Thinking in Systems* for the first time while studying agricultural and food law. Encountering it altered far more than just her career path; it shifted what she was capable of perceiving and understanding about the world around her and renewed her faith in our ability to live lives of meaning and impact.

However, as with any good magic, there was a price to be paid. Once you start thinking about systems, you will see systems everywhere and you won't be able to unsee them. You'll quickly realize that no system exists in isolation – so you'll start wondering where one system ends and another begins. The answer may well be everywhere and nowhere. (Overwhelming! And, of course, you can't ever know everything about everything.) So, sketching in some boundaries is necessary for our human brains to actually sense-make and do some analysis.

The food system is especially vast and encompassing – it touches and connects to just about everything. At the widest span and at some very specific points, food systems interact with land, air, water, and living beings. In natural science terms, that means they draw from and influence all four spheres of the Earth: the geosphere, hydrosphere, atmosphere, and biosphere.

In more human terms, food systems interact with and influence our economies, politics, social arrangements, health systems, cultures, and bodies. They involve the movement of pulses from India to Iceland and the movement of morsels from bowls to bowels. What's more, everyone eats – so we all participate in, depend upon, and are inherently familiar with some parts of the food system.

We all have a stake in the food system, many ways into it, and frequent opportunities to shape change in and through food. This makes food systems change or alteration really powerful. But it can also make the whole thing unwieldy and overwhelming, so in the food systems field, we create maps and models of "the food system," aware that we are always making choices (and not always consciously) about what to include and exclude as parts of the system. Meadows urges us to "remember that boundaries are of our own making, and that they can and should be reconsidered for each new discussion, problem, or purpose."

Throughout our lives and careers, we've found food systems maps – colorful, arrow-festooned attempts to visualize the elements, interactions, stocks and flows of the food system – to be at once overly complicated and utterly insufficient. But, that's not really the fault of the graphic designers. The most relevant parts of a system shift based on the questions we are asking about it. And now that we're asking questions about the nature of the relationships that shape the system and its self-organizing patterns, parts that might make it onto a food system map drawn by an investor, a supply chain manager, or even an environmental scientist may need to recede, while other parts – the interconnections – are suddenly more salient and need more prominent representation.

Interconnections Shape Change

One of Donella Meadow's keenest insights is that changing the elements of a system rarely changes the system's behavior.

This is because the interconnections within the system (the feedbacks and incentives) will drive new elements to behave similarly in accordance with the system's purpose. In other words, the system's structure can overpower the individuality of the elements. So, to shape change within a system, we must examine the interconnections – or in our parlance, the relationships and the culture. Fashioning new relationships and changing the culture is how we change the behavior of a system. The most consequential changes in system redesign are those that "improve the information, incentives, disincentives, goals, stresses, and constraints"[2] that affect the elements.

Focusing on the interconnections means that there are many places to intervene in complex systems – and the intervening need not be done only by those with the greatest levels of formal power, the strongest voice, or the biggest bully pulpit. Taking this a step further, we need to change the culture that shapes the relationships and goals of the food system, because it is the most elegant and also the most accessible way to go about the work we propose. This is good news: it means that we can all participate in making the food system we want. (But not necessarily by following popular food movement advice about "voting with our forks" or "paying the true cost of food." Such advice might alter the amount and direction of money flowing through the system, which is an element, but not the nature of the connections themselves.)

Systems theorists get really excited about what they call "leverage points" – places to intervene within a complex system where a small shift in one thing has the potential to produce big changes in everything. We get excited about them, too, for the same reason that Nicole's kids get excited about the zany engineering of Rube Goldberg machines: Whoa, doing this over here makes that happen all the way over there!? And there? And there, too? But on the flip side of that excitement lies some trepidation. If we identify a leverage point, how do we know what to do with it? Which way to push the lever? How much force will it take? What happens if we act on a leverage point – especially in something that is as big a deal as the food system – without recognizing it as such? Will the unintended consequences cause more harm than good?

Because the food system(s) are so dynamic, complex, and interconnected, there is no way of ever being sure. The lack of certainty, though, doesn't give us a free pass to fuck around and find out. (Though this seems to be exactly how the agrichemical and meat industry titans have approached food systems experimentation – with their products and production models that drive massive monoculture, intensive industrialization, cramped consolidation and produce, among other ills, superweeds, superbugs, and dead zones.)

This is, in fact, why we need sets of principles or ethics to guide our actions and guard against the worst outcomes. We will introduce those principles in Chapter Four, once we have mapped out and analyzed the problems. Then, you will be able to put it all together with more context.

For us, relationality does a good bit of that important guiding work – but then in relationship, we must grapple together with the "shoulds" and "should nots" (ethical inquiry), take an honest look at "what is" and "what if" (ground-truthing and imagining) and attempt together to find moves that bridge rather than break (building new interconnections).

Perhaps the most sage piece of advice that Donella Meadows left us with is permission to dance: "We can't control systems or figure them out. But we can dance with them! Living successfully in a world of systems requires more of us than our ability to calculate. It requires our full humanity – our rationality, our ability to sort out truth from falsehood, our intuition, our compassion, our vision, and our morality."[3] Donella Meadows is not alone in thinking change is a dance. One of our favorite activists and spiritual badasses,

Reginald Hubbard agrees. He says "I don't want to be part of a movement that doesn't dance."

Making Change, Feeling Trouble

In order to create change in any system, we need to stay present with the reality of what we know. This is doubly true in the food system because you really don't have any choice. It's not a system you can easily exit – at least not if you'd like to stay alive.

Staying rooted in place and staying with the reality of what we know is happening to food systems and the natural world means seeing and having a relationship with what we will call "trouble." People do not want to "stay with the trouble" as the feminist philosopher Donna Haraway puts it in her book *Staying with the Trouble: Making Kin in the Chtulucene*. It is so much easier to deny it. Just look at how some people – especially those with lots of economic or political power and a strong status-quo bias – have reacted to overwhelming evidence of climate change and its human causation: fossil fuel magnates covering up the evidence and blaming volcanoes, politicians turning a crisis into jokes about the weather, and retailers over-emphasizing narrow and illusory benefits. Others want to leap ahead, as if it were possible to dodge an unprecedented planetary crisis. Some put their energy into as-yet unproven techno-utopian solutions. Others spend their billionaire winnings on space-man fantasies and ill-conceived Mars missions, failing to recognize that colonization plus capitalism already added up to a whole lot of climate crisis on a far more human-friendly planet. Finally, some people just give up and give themselves over to grief – a tempting response to what feels like a hopeless situation. But submissive surrender has a dangerous viral quality – it is all too easy to transmit that shut-down feeling to others. And immobilized masses aren't good at making radical alternative futures into realities.

Denial, deception, and overwhelm are natural responses in a system addicted to greed and surplus accumulation. They are understandable responses to dehumanizing, denaturing forces that treat life and this precious planet's capacity to support it as disposable. These responses, in fact, make it possible to stay in a system that will kill us. They also isolate us – either by separating us from reality, from each other, or from our own passion and will to live creatively. They make us compliant or at least shut us up. So we absolutely must circumvent these culturally appropriate and conditioned responses if we are to make any kind of change.

Culture change is often ignored when people who study the environment, food systems, and economic inequality begin to spin out their "solutions." Culture – the learned and expressed beliefs, values, and assumptions that groups of people share and consider valid ways of understanding the world – is handed down across generations, but it is also dynamic and changeable. Like cultivation, which shares the same linguistic root, culture is a process. Culture is created by relationships, through the stories we tell each other, and in our bodies. Culture is in all of us, not outside us, and it informs all of our ideas, actions, and decisions. Inattention to culture, and especially to the dominant or overculture, is a key reason that good ideas veer away from their intended impact as they are implemented. Shifting culture is just about the most powerful way to shift the leverage points Donella Meadows talks about. If we don't shift culture, we simply will not succeed and may not survive. We cannot cast seeds of change on saline soil and think they will germinate.

Making change, any change, involves altering the way we look at the world around us. We are creating alternate realities out of the same stuff of life that was always in front of us. This is one reason change is hard. We are primed to see the world one way, and when asked to tilt our heads and squint to see it differently, we're resistant.

Change is also hard because we are usually asked to do it when things are bad, when we are experiencing a traumatic event, or when we are at the end of our rope. Stress puts us into protective mode, not learning mode. Stress prevents us from being receptive to and playful with new ideas. It makes us queasy, not curious when we peer out over the edge of the unknown. We want safety. We want familiarity – even when the familiar is tied up with our suffering. The late Thich Nhat Hanh said "People have a hard time letting go of their suffering. Out of a fear of the unknown, they prefer suffering that is familiar." The wind of new ideas blowing through our hair feels precarious, and we already have more than enough precarity.

We cannot make the changes we need from a place where we are still mired in the thinking, ideas, systems, and assumptions that created the problems in the food system, the ones we will outline in the next chapter. Everyone from Albert Einstein, who may have said "We can't solve problems by using the same kind of thinking we used when we created them," to the writer Audre Lorde, who wrote an essay named "The Master's Tools Will Never Dismantle the Master's House," agree that cultural and paradigm shifts (by this we mean toward relationships, of course) are needed for change to stick.

We are not going to pummel you with a lot of technological or technocratic fixes for the food system, though we might mention some. We are not going to find the magic food product that will feed the world and persuade you that it is our only hope and then sell it to you. And, we are definitely not going to fetishize the market because we believe deeply that the addiction to extractive practices, greed, supremacy, and endless growth that we experience as late-stage capitalism is part of the problem.

What we propose is a movement to change the interconnections in the food system across a spectrum, away from transactional interactions towards relational ones, away from competition and towards collaboration, away from consumption and towards reciprocity, away from extraction and towards empathy, and away from global and towards *cosmolocal*.

(Cosmolocalism, which we will delve into in Chapter Four, offers a way to keep the best bits of global connections while limiting the parts that hollow out local communities, homogenize cultures, and make our material lives unnecessarily and dangerously distant and complex.)

When our view becomes relational, the kinds of changes we make will sustain us and change the system. They will be substantive enough to reshape our world.

What Won't Work

Here are some things that will not "fix" the food system. The items on this list may surprise you. We like some of these things and are deeply skeptical of others. But, they all share a commonality: when enacted in an extractive, transactional, competitive, global and neoliberal capitalist system, none of these "solutions" are likely to make much difference at all: regenerative agriculture, more organic certification, third party green labeling and certifications, fair trade, mandating veganism, cellular agriculture, golden rice, hacking photosynthesis, indoor and or vertical farming, soilless agriculture, GMOs, agri-robotics, big data solutions, farmers' markets, food recovery, composting, urban agriculture, biopesticides, and aquaculture.

Some of these could, when enacted relationally, absolutely move us in the right direction. But no one of them is so heavy-duty that, when they are introduced into the machine of extractive capitalism, would jam the works, prevent extraction, end supremacy and inequality, and save us. We are not going to find an end to hunger inside the system that maintains it. And we are not going to solve any of the problems we will copiously list in Chapter Two if we keep thinking we can save extractive capitalism at the same time. As Raj Patel and Jason W. Moore have proven in their *book A History of the World in Seven Cheap Things*, capitalism is not just an economic system but a "way of organizing the relations between humans and the rest of nature."

So, we must all work together to reorganize the relations. We'll equip you to exist within a new paradigm so that as you make choices and changes, you can reorganize relations in ways that allow life to thrive. Small voices can change the values that drive those interconnections in the system to move together along the spectrum towards relationship, empathy, collaboration, and cosmolocalism.

None of us can do it perfectly, and certainly not while extraction and supremacy working through capitalism are steering the ship. That's okay, we don't need to. Perfectionism is an invasive species in our minds. It is like the Asian lady beetles coming into the house this week while we edit, who were first introduced to the region to control an aphid problem but now have no predators. They seem endless, stinky, and no matter how many we vacuum up, there is a new one on the desk when we look down. If you have hard tendencies toward the perfect, try to remember that perfectionism was introduced into our minds by White supremacy, patriarchy, capitalism, and human domination. That usually makes it easier to let go of. Better yet, let's vacuum up perfectionism (as we have been doing with the beetles) and compost it.

For example, we both plan to keep drinking coffee and eating chocolate until it is not possible – forever if we make a cosmolocal trade arrangement possible. We believe in local food systems. Luckily we also believe nothing is all black and white. So we do what we can and we look for better ideas for the rest. And we will live under capitalism as long as it is here, making as many of the best choices we can while meeting our needs. We'll just do it wearing the T-shirt that quotes the science fiction genius Ursula Le Guin: "We live in Capitalism – Its power seems inescapable but so did the divine right of kings." We don't need a perfect world or to be perfect people (or professionals) to make progress. In fact, being flexible and forgiving in the present prepares us for living new futures. It's how we escape.

The futures we need are already appearing around us. If anyone tells you this is pie in the sky naive talk, we say it's not because we have seen, participated in, read about, and been told stories that illustrate the change is possible, and in fact, already here. In Chapter Five, we will visit those futures where they are blooming so that we can put together a working vision of change – one you can actually imagine working in your place and community.

Preparing to Enter the Relational Paradigm

Our process and proposal for saving the food system and the planet is deceptively simple: Move towards relationship.

Because relationality is not how those interconnections in the food system work today, many of us have been living for several generations (but not for all of human history, nor in every place or community, which is important to remember) in a system that breaks connection on purpose, that isolates us, and keeps us from rooting deeply where we are planted. Making that relational shift requires both tools and fences. We use these to build refuges in which relational culture can root.

A move toward relationship is not even a novel solution. In fact, articulating it requires us to be as relational in our theory as we aim to be in our practice. Our theorizing draws from fields as diverse as computer science, science fiction, sociology, feminist philosophy, ecology, indigenous studies, narratology, biology, feminism, economics, critical studies, ethnography, theology, political science, gastronomy, mycology, geography, urban studies, community organizing, organizational development, psychology, neurobiology, comparative literature, ethics, agriculture, animal husbandry, critical race theory, legal studies, and agronomy. We bring them into relationship with each other to create our own transcontinental cosmolocal paradigm for sustenance and thriving. In more simple terms, we know that we can't change the world with the ideas we could produce alone. We recognize a need to be in relationship both within our own fields and then with wider and wider circles of thinking and practice.

Our writing collaboration is, for us, a symbiotic relational undertaking. We are both so rooted in our fields that we need the other person's knowledge and perspective to create something comprehensive. As we spin out new lines of thinking, one or the other of us will often laugh and say, "I don't even know what that word means!" As we slow down and explain ideas that the other person has never heard of, we are bridging fields, ways of thinking, and personalities. This kind of exchange is essential to create anything that is encompassing and specific enough to address problems that were spawned globally but manifest locally. Problems that impact spheres as intimate as our bodies and as shared as the planet we all inhabit. We are also in deeply appreciative relationship with all the people we quote in this book. Their ideas, hearts, minds, and words are gifts offered with no expectation of immediate exchange in return. In sharing the ways they make sense of the world, they've pieced together whole sections of the puzzle we've been working on. How could we not love them for this? We would go as far as to say that nothing we, or any other thinkers, say is ever truly individual. We believe ideas, theories, concepts and even thoughts are relational and no one, even if they tell you otherwise, ever came up with one in some individualistic isolation. Just as we are a part of a relational network, so are our ideas and we celebrate that.

Building Our Change Competence

People making relational changes in the interconnections of the food system need to be change competent, and we suspect that many of us aren't. However, change competence is made up of a few skills we already know how to cultivate. Getting there is a matter of practice, not unlike learning how to cook. Nicole's kids are just learning how to cook, so she is teaching them the basics: knife skills, how to use an oven and a stove, how to flavor foods with herbs and spices. They are learning to make the food Nicole likes and would cook. Michelle's kids are adults living away from home, and as they moved on to cook for themselves, they didn't need to learn to use a knife all over again, instead they needed to take skills they already had and apply them in new ways with the new ingredients available to them and to create foods they love. The transition was rough as each of them learned that this or that ingredient wasn't available where they live or they wanted to recreate something they loved from home but didn't have the right equipment. It was awkward and uncomfortable, but because eating is not optional, they figured it out. They still call home for recipe suggestions regularly, but now out of love and connection and not for any kind of help with the discomfort.

Change competence includes three skills. The first skill in change competence is the ability to be uncomfortable. The second is the power to stay in place long enough for the magical process to happen. The third skill is relating what you know to people near and far.

Boiled way down like syrup:

(1) tolerate discomfort or *be in the trouble*
(2) stay to shift or *stay rooted in place*
(3) relate or *share our stories*

Humans long ago developed a technology that does all three of these things, so you will not need to take the steps individually. That said, it is helpful to understand each of them before we move on.

Be in the Trouble

Change doesn't happen without trouble. Trouble is, for us, a technical term. It's the stuff that happens to us or that we create as we move through life that ends up changing us or changing the world. And we are now in very troubling times. When people say shit happens, what they mean is trouble happens. Trouble is like churning butter. We have milk, then we have this agitating churning process that feels messy and takes so long we think we will never end up with anything useful. Finally, a coherent lump of wonderfulness comes together; the unnecessary parts are strained out and saved for other endeavors. Most people don't love the feeling of trouble, but the ability to ride out the churn is essential to change. We are, according to Buddhist teacher angel kyodo williams, bad at discomfort and therefore not able to change.[4] The solution williams suggests is based in her Buddhist practice, which is one way to address being willing to sit still with the uncomfortable feelings.

The skills in this part of the change process are to learn to be in your body while you are feeling stuff you'd rather not. As the great thinker and writer Octavia Butler puts it in the *Parable of the Sower*: "The only lasting truth is change." And we mostly hate change. So while we need to be looking around us gathering the information we need from as many places, people, and ideas as we can, we need to be able to live in the discomfort and the trouble. Like bees going out to look for nectar, we need to be willing to go way outside our comfort zone to find out what reality is and be able to manage our body, feelings, and mental states.

When we are not able to face into trouble, we create coping mechanisms that make us selfish, self-seeking, petty, quick to judgment, and closed-minded. In other words, we respond from trauma rather than healing. If we don't practice being uncomfortable, we will end up displacing our discomfort onto the planet, ecosystems, and other people. We see this in all the "isms" and phobias we have practiced on each other: racism, sexism, ableism, and the list goes on. While it is oversimplified to say that they are "just" the outcomes of being unwilling to be uncomfortable, they are certainly one of the more destructive manifestations. They are creating separation to avoid discomfort, or in the words of john powell, professor and bridge builder, they are breaking when we need to be bridging.[5]

Some of this discomfort we are, and will be, experiencing in our relationship with the food system will come from the changes that ecological crisis, species depletion, and climate change will bring us. Some of the discomfort will come from reckoning with harms we have created in the past. An unmissable part of weaving more worthy food systems is attending to our collective obligation to undo harms. We engage in redemption in food systems by reckoning with history, revealing its reverberations today, and rebalancing power. This is uncomfortable work and when we displace that discomfort, we make it worse for the people already most harmed.

Being able to be in trouble and even go out and find new trouble you didn't know about and still feel, think, and act without reflexively reacting, retrenching, or creating more harm is skill number one.

Stay Rooted in Place

The second skill is the power to stay in place. When we stay in place we can start to build networks, relationships, and change. We can go through processes and see things shift and morph. If we fight, flee, or otherwise break instead of staying put, we cannot reap any of the benefits of change. Donna Haraway offers "making odd kin" as a way of staying with the trouble, noting that "we require each other in unexpected collaborations and combinations, in hot compost piles. We become – with each other or not at all."[6]

Being rooted in place is a process of composting. All sorts of elements stay in relationship with each other long enough that processes can happen and what was scrap becomes nourishing soil. We need to become relational, communal, collaborative, empathic, and connected and we cannot do that if trouble makes us move, run, turn away, or give up. We have to stay put, stay open, stay flexible, and stay in the game. To go back to our bees who gathered pollen while seeking nectar, this is the process of that pollen becoming food. It takes time, a very specific place, and a set of processes.

If we don't stay rooted we end up "pulling a geographic" (which means moving to a new place in an attempt to solve problems internal to us) and thinking that a new place or context will make us different people. We skip around, looking at problem after problem and having an initial spark of interest but not staying put long enough for any change process to occur. And in this phase, we need processes to unfold. In other words, we need to care longer. We cannot change all the leverage points in a system ourselves. We need other change shapers in order to make substantive transformation, no matter how important we think we are. Humility and relationality tell us that we need each other and we better get used to it.

To shape this change, we first need to have a set of emotional skills that allows us to be uncomfortable; then, we need to develop them so we endure. Stay longer. Consider longer. Care longer. By expanding our window of tolerance for trouble, we become available to more change. Climate crisis and collapse amplify urgency in very real ways, but they do not displace the need to cultivate this skill. If we rush our responses, they simply won't be butter (or honey). The churning process, the compost process, the gestation process, the connection process, the processes that turn that nectar into honey, water cycles, even something as basic as digestion are not instant. They are most successful when you let nature get on with itself and you stay part of it.

Share Our Stories

Once we have learned all these lessons from the trouble and through staying in place, we need to share them across communities or in our community across time. We need to relate. But sharing change can be tricky: What worked for us might not work for someone or somewhere else. The way we share our learnings might turn others off, scare them, or shut them down. Have you ever loved a song, a movie, or a kind of food so much that you told everyone about it and people got sick of hearing you talk about it and ignored the very thing you loved because of how you could not shut up about it? It's hard to share transformational moments or processes without blunting the impact by either turning it into a prescription or data. To streamline the telling and prove impact, we often season with shoulds and pureé our experiences into data. Neither work. Telling people what to do brings up resistance. Data, alone and out of context, can fall flat or be manipulated. Overzealous promises can underdeliver. Telling people how to feel about something might even incline them toward the opposite just out of stubbornness or status quo. Most frustratingly, the import of our innovation might be written off by people who don't want to see the looming trouble.

Story Technology

This is where story comes in. Story is a technology as old as humanity. Either our brains were formed by it or we created it based on how our brains work, making it the most well adapted technology for sharing complex change information. Story helped people find plants and animals they needed to survive, it was used to explain natural cycles so that people could cultivate food and thrive, it created community, and we still crave it. There is such a strong human pull toward sitting around a fire and sharing stories that we still do it. But now the "firelight" comes from a screen and the stories are transmitted digitally.[7]

Story also functions to help us learn things we don't want to or need to learn firsthand. This is called surrogate scenario building. Stories provide the opportunity for individuals to understand scenarios we just can't afford to try out on our own. Should each person try to figure out which mushrooms are poisonous, or would it be better to receive hard-won lessons from others? If we don't create our stories as a gift to each other and to our system, our experience stays isolated and withers instead of propagating like wild strawberries. Wild strawberries reproduce with runners coming out of the mother plant, allowing daughter plants to spring up in new locations. These connections don't last forever but they certainly spread the sweet red berries efficiently. The mother plant can photosynthesize for the daughter plants while they are growing but eventually they don't need the mother. Wild strawberries also produce seeds so they can reproduce in more than one way. That about sums up how stories diffuse change.

Change does not last if there is no diffusion of innovation. It needs to move from a place where it worked to new places where it's needed, either via runners or seeds, from community to community. When we expand on our ideas about cosmolocalism and targeted universalism in a later chapter, you will shake your head yes. The idea that we shape change, then share it and spark both interest and possibility in others just feels so right – it is how we change becomes possible in systems that feel huge and unwieldy (because they are).

Our Stories Shape Change
and Stretch Our Relational Skills

These three skills sound like they would take years to develop, and they have. Millenia, in fact. However, over the millennia, every human wisdom tradition has figured them out, be it angel kyodo william's Buddhism or the Sufism we learn from poetry, or the mosque, synagogue, church down the street, or the healing and herbal traditions passed down through lineages of practitioners. Wisdom or faith traditions all have had the same challenges: share truth as they see it, inspire belief and then action in their people, change thinking and behavior, transmit this belief and change across generations, support people in times of crisis, face hardship, persist against injustice, and create community while doing all of the above.

The technology they all use? Story. Because this simple but universal piece of technology holds so much and does so many jobs, we often overlook it. We think of it as entertainment. Then, we get duped because it is working in our brains, regardless of whether we grant it the respect it deserves.

We don't need to "teach" you story skills in this book, but we do want to make you very aware that you need them. Whole books exist on this and whole classes and even certificate programs. For the sake of your change shaping, culture making, and relationship building there are a few things to know. If you do want to consciously work on those skills you can take a look at Michelle's book *Resilience: The Life Saving Skill of Story* or the Story Justice course in EcoGather.

The Ways Story Works

Story is simple. You need a character with whom you will develop an emotional attachment (empathy), a plot (trouble happening to the character that they will work through), and a resolution (that helps you learn individually). When we have those three simple components, our brains are sucked in. Research has shown that people will give more money, believe new things, change opinions, feel connected, keep the changes for weeks if not years, when we learn through story.[8] We need the parts of our brain that story activates for making decisions, for understanding other people, and for seeing possibilities.

Stories create empathy by putting a character with whom you form an attachment through trouble. Empathy is sometimes given a bad name because we think of it as "feeling sorry" for someone without wanting to get involved or do anything. That is not the empathy we are talking about. Our version of empathy is what is called "thick" empathy which is being in community with each other, showing up for each other, and having each other's backs.[9] This is what both Donna Haraway and Patty Krawec (among others) each talk about, in their own ways, as becoming kin.[10] We need to activate our brains to feel with other people, communities, our environment, the plants and animals and people in the food system, and the Earth itself.

A very simple example is the rat in the movie *Ratatouille*. Never before have so many people felt so good about knowing there was a rat interacting with their food than after watching that movie. It doesn't matter that our logic tells us vermin are touching the food, our empathic response is to root for the rat.

The empathy supplied by stories breathes life into data and cloaks it in context. No one makes decisions from data alone. When we get to deciding, the emotional centers in our brain light up.[11] And when we encounter data without a story, we are apt to make one up. This isn't pernicious; it is just how our brains work – they gap-fill to sense-make.[12] Thus, by delivering data in a (non-manipulative) story-based context, the problems of data-driven misinformation and disinformation can be reduced. In other words, it is harder to misrepresent or manipulate data when you also provide the context in a story.

Stories also help us practice being and staying with trouble because they stimulate in our bodies the feelings we might have if the trouble were happening to us. Our bodies respond, we successfully manage it, and our capacity grows. Plus, our awareness expands as we feel and understand the positive outcomes of a difficult story. This, again, is what we called surrogate scenario building. Having had a positive outcome demonstrated, we are better able to appreciate the necessity of staying with the trouble.

Stories are particularly useful for communicating across difference. Unlike competing facts or versions of reality, stories circumvent the parts of our brains that prejudge facts and arguments. When we use story to share our experience, our hopes, or our developed strengths, we offer people possibilities and new ways of thinking. When we tell people how to practice, what to do, and how to think, it is all too easy to rebel, argue, disagree.

Loren Cardeli and his organization, A Growing Culture, use storytelling as one of the key components of their change shaping work, which endeavors to address power disparities in the food system and center the peasant food web. "We believe stories are at the heart of systems change. Our storytelling confronts the root causes of injustice in our food system and centers the communities, seeding radical hope for a just and dignified future for all."[13] Their Hunger for Justice is a storytelling series that uses the power of story to shift the dialogue away from the symptoms and data about the problem to the roots of the problem. They call their platform emergent (we will talk about emergence in Chapter Five) and use it as an interactive way for movements making food systems change to connect. They know the power of the story to bridge and to help us draw more holistic conclusions.

In fact, we have used food as a feast, a sacrifice, medicine, and for celebration since at least 600 BCE with each culture from China to Greece to Persia to India to Africa telling stories about how we fit into the cosmos through food. Food prohibitions tell their own stories about creating community and knowing who is in and who is out. We feasted with the Gods and fasted for humility, and we fed each other the cosmos on a plate. When rulers in the ancient world wanted to extend their power, they fed people because those who feed you gain your appreciation. There are so many stories told with and about food that this book is full of them. We will share people, ideas, history, personal stories, and cultural ones as we go. And from them you can draw your own conclusions, as that is the beauty of story.

Stories we tell come from both the past and the future. We will talk about stories from the future as a way to play out outcomes and possibilities in Chapter Three. Stories from the past come to us from all kinds of disciplines: faith and wisdom stories, anthropology, history, family tales, and cultural narratives. They reveal deep ancestral truths that we really must remember if we are to break the spell of the current overculture. Ancient stories tell us that humans did not always organize themselves as we do today. We did not always live this way. And in fact, human nature is not the competitive, avaricious perversion we've come to think of it as. Thomas Hobbes' dismal insistence that we never cooperate unless compelled against our will and our natural state results inevitably in war is more assertion than evidence. The anthropological and historical records – along with plenty of stories from diverse wisdom traditions – reveal that we were not always primarily preoccupied with the self to the detriment of the community. Humans, by nature, crave kinship and find belonging in a band, a family, a tribe because we simply cannot survive for long outside a group.

Supremacy of the individual and competitive orientation are recent constructs that suit and serve extractive and neoliberal capitalism and the notion of nation states – constructs that evade examination and consolidate power when they are presented with an air of inevitability and accepted as "human nature." Modern humans have grown so accustomed to seeing this fun-house mirror reflection of ourselves that we actually believe the distortion to be real. No wonder we move through the world with exaggerated senses of self. This leads some theorists to posit that humans are now products of the modern nation state and the economic systems that control them.

Stories from humans long past remind us that this moment in time is not forever or always. Just as we can use story to make new futures, we can also use it to get right with our past and the possibilities it endorses. Our friend Shaun Chamberlin, who you will meet in Chapter Three, puts it this way "[I]t's demonstrably not 'simply human nature' to annihilate all around us. No, it's the nature of this particular human culture. Human potential is so much more, and that's why conflating the two is so toxic."[14]

Because our take-aways from a story are the lessons we draw out ourselves, stories become a stage, a laboratory, a thought experiment, a scenario building exercise, or a sensory experience. When done right they don't moralize, force their point, or tell us what to think. We come to our own conclusions and we are much less likely to question our own conclusions than those forced down our throats.

Throughout that entire process, story fosters relationship. We share, are vulnerable, and transmit feelings across space. We listen, are open and honest, we willingly take in another person. Those are the very relational skills we need to move from transaction (data, money, facts, if you do X, then I'll do Y) to relationship (I understand you and what you experienced and have learned from it).

When change happens fast, as it does in food and other human systems, we experience unease and anxiety. We can respond to anxiety in a number of ways; john a. powell, who directs the Othering and Belonging Institute at U.C. Berkeley says that the narratives we hear influence our response to change. When we hear narratives that separate us from others (be they people, the land, or other species), we experience breaking. Connections sever, our attention pulls in, and our focus shifts to the self, which feels more comfortable. For instance, we hear a lot about how jobs are moving to India and other "offshore" locations, purportedly leaving Americans worse off. Often those jobs and the people who hold them are blamed or looked down upon. For this and many other reasons people have developed antipathy towards these offshore workers. If we hear narratives that help us see other interests, values and beings as real, multi-faceted, and interesting, we are moved to bridge the distance and work with them. Compelled by her deep love of Indian regional cuisine, Michelle unintentionally began using customer service calls to learn more about cooking. When she found out she was talking to someone in India, she would conduct the business of the call with anticipation because as soon as it was over she would hurriedly ask: "What's your favorite dish your mother makes?" In response, the call center employee would lower their voice and start talking really fast, describing a home meal and even offering to provide recipes. Though an ocean apart, this bridging conversation humanizes both parties and often ends with laughter and exchanging email addresses. In his talks about breaking and bridging, john powell makes a point we love – that values, cares, culture, and goals are what bring us together across difference to solve problems and we get there through story.[15]

Indigenous Communities: Stories, Food, and Place

Stories help us learn and tend a place, enabling us to become a part of it. Across generations, indigenous peoples have used stories to share knowledge, hone identity and transmit a lineage of wisdom based on a particular place, its ecosystems, and the spirits or energies in it. This kind of story is the end result of staying rooted in one place. When change creeps in and people need to alter their relationship to the food system, such stories offer a well of experience and tradition from which to draw.

Food activist, chef, and restaurateur Selassie Atadika uses food to tell cultural stories that create changes in foodways for more resilient communities in Ghana where she lives and works. She uses food like yams, soursop, and groundnut to tell cultural and historical stories that have never been written down but that are universally a part of her community. She then leans into these stories to improve supply chains, health conditions, and other feed-related outcomes.

In an interview, Selassie said she demonstrates on the plate what deep rootedness and connection can bring to a community, even when the world around them is changing. She says that she shows the food and explains how it supports certain value chains, but then she always adds a twist to help people deconstruct what they know and learn new ways of feeding and nourishing themselves. "We don't have a lot of written history in Ghana about our foodways. So a lot of my food comes from my childhood and my grandmother and my Auntie's childhood stories. I'll talk to everybody who will talk to me, getting them to explain to me what and how they eat and then trying to understand from the information they share with me. I start to understand why they eat or have been eating a certain type of way. And then, when I put it on the plate, I show it back in a story, and I use that story about our food to inform my community but I even use it when I cook for people far away, like when I was in Colorado visiting and cooking. I'm able to tell stories through the food. And it helps people to understand the importance of these different elements on the plate and how community, culture, and cuisine are intersecting with environmental sustainability in the economy, because that's actually the circularity that we have there. And we need to allow all those pieces to show."[16]

Not all of us have the privilege of living where our people were indigenous, though. Many of the folks originally indigenous to one place are now living in diaspora.

Diasporic Communities: Stories, Food, and Change

We are not the first people to take up the task of navigating major changes. Nor are we the first to have the responsibility to deal with change foisted upon us. Change has been a part of human evolution as far back as we can trace. Diasporic communities and people – those forced by politics, genocide, famine, xenophobia, racism, economic collapse, war, and enslavement to leave the place where they (or the ancestors) were indigenous – know some things about the complete change of context and revision of culture that we're exploring in this book. After displacement or migration, nothing is the same and the circumstances are rarely about choice. So how do those communities evolve their identities, maintain their relationality, and yet become, as indigenous ecologist Robin Wall Kimmerer talks about, naturalized to a new place?[17]

Two practices of diasporic communities demonstrate how relationship can serve as a balancing and stabilizing force that allows settling gently into and eventually becoming naturalized to a place.[18] The first, not surprisingly, is foodways. Cooking, growing, sourcing, and creating the foods and experiences make a bridge between their present-place and their homeland. Familiar ingredients, combinations, and techniques – as well as evocative flavors, textures, and aromas – conjure a sense of home long before (and after) one might feel comfortable applying the word to the new context.

The second practice is story – as both a carrier of generational and life histories, information, tools, ideas, and mindsets, and a way for distinguishing what was and what is. Eating familiar foods helps diasporic peoples to metabolize change: they can draw strength from their origins and process their new environs. Sharing stories also offers a way of metabolizing trauma, converting it into survival and resilience.

The work of Hazon, the largest faith-based climate change organization in the world, leads a diasporic community to make relational choices and changes in their institutions that will result in more sustainable food systems, communities, and environment. In their sustainability seal program they ask a diasporic community, the broad range of people who make up the Jewish community after having been displaced from a range of countries and local food systems, to make another change, to reduce food waste amongst other environmental choices, this time in the place they have landed.

Becky O'Brien, Hazon's Director of Food & Climate told Michelle about how she uses story when she helps communities through the discomfort of trying to make sustainable changes to the way a community cooks and serves food in their religious institutions. She says she ran up against really panicked people who had used food, up to that point, to settle themselves and connect themselves to their pasts. She found that first, before asking for any kind of change, she needed to let people tell their food stories, about what their grandmothers baked and what they ate as children that had been passed down over generations. After people assured themselves that they had held on to their culture, she asked them to tell stories about what it was like for their ancestors to find and cook food in a new place – what hardships they encountered and what lessons they learned. Then, and only then, could she move them into an exploration of how they could change the way they now cooked and served people in their synagogues, with an eye toward sustainability. Traversing their intergenerational history of adaptation reminded people of what they are capable of and the stories pollinated new change.

As we move forward through the book, please keep in mind both indigenous and diasporic sources of strength, information, change agility, and future building – we will need them to deal with the damage we see in the system and in the solutions we create.

Chapter 2

The Damaging – Not Broken – Global Food System

Too many food systems articles, books, and courses open with a catalog of calamities or inventory of injustices. We resisted that impulse because we know that view makes the food system appear more like a tangled snare than a web of relationships. Instead, we have tried to prepare you to see the system and stay with the trouble – and we are promising you a set of compelling dispatches from a relational future in Chapters Four and Five. But, for now, we absolutely must do some reckoning together about the food system. If we've crafted this well, it shouldn't feel like trauma tourism – our aim is not to overwhelm you with the awfulness of it all, but to allow you to see the many sharp facets and wounding edges of the systems that are supposed to nourish and sustain human life. As we fold data into the story, you'll start to see that the global food system we have isn't one we want or can afford to keep.

Before we go any further, it is probably worth aligning on what a "food system" is. Remember, a system is defined as: "an interconnected set of elements that is coherently organized in a way that achieves something."[19] Accordingly, we define a food system as *an interconnected web of people, coexistent species, resources, and activities that extend across all domains involved in providing human nourishment, supporting vitality, and expressing comestible culture.* With vitality – the capacity to live, grow, or develop – right there in the definition, it is plain that the food system is concerned with enabling the maintenance of human lives. Because humans are generally interested in the continuance of their species (even if we don't always act like it), our food systems ought to be concerned not only with sustenance for current generations, but also with sustaining their own ability to function and continue providing for human food needs indefinitely without fouling or threatening other essentials for life, such as clean water and breathable air.

Functionally, each food system encompasses knowledge, energy, inputs, production, processing, packaging, distribution, marketing, consumption, disposal, valorization or circular reintegration of food. Adaptive, self-organizing features of food systems reflect, respond to, and subsequently influence historical, social, cultural, political, economic, health, and environmental conditions and power relations. Sometimes it is helpful to conceive of a singular food system; here we also recognize that there are many nested and interconnected food systems (plural). And, each of them is a potential site for a relational shift.

Food systems all have some common components: inputs, agricultural production (and/or capture and forage), processing or preservation, transportation, preparation, consumption, residual and waste management, technology, and exchanges. But, because food systems can be identified and operate at multiple scales from a household or institution to a city, region, nation, or entire world, what those components look like, how complex and diverse they are, and how many lives they involve or serve vary widely.

For example, on the shelves of the local grocery store where Michelle shops, and Nicole used to shop, is coffee from a local roastery run by a lovely man and coffee nerd named Josh Crane. Josh sources the coffee he sells in a relational way, through direct trade. He's super intentional about cutting out the extra hands that take profit from the coffee. He lowers the complexity of the system through the choices he makes (we will get to that later). Josh roasts the coffee down the road at his roastery, The Coffee Ride, and delivers it by bike to both grocery stores and people's homes. So, when Josh hands Michelle a bag of coffee, he knows the people who grew it, he roasted it, packaged it and delivered it. Josh loves to talk about coffee, and he is always open to input. Michelle was finding a coffee he made too light and acidic and she explained to him when he handed her a bag that the last one she bought didn't work for her. Josh came back the next week and said, "I roasted the coffee for an extra minute and I think you'll like it better," and shoved a bag of coffee at her. It was much, much better.

The ability to impact a small part of the local food system was immediate. Because the complexity was lower, the relationship was a leverage point. Now, relationality is Josh's business model anyhow; he is always trying to lower the complexity and increase the relationality.

Comparing this exchange to commodity coffee supply chains reveals a lot about how the global food system typically takes shape. The elixir that powers us through modern life gets its start when farmers cultivate woody shrubs of the *coffea* genus, typically at high altitudes in equatorial regions. Several years after planting, these shrubs burst into fragrant flower and produce clusters of green coffee cherries. After hand-harvesting the ripe red cherries, coffee farmers will either pulp, wash, dry, and sort the cherries themselves, do so as part of a collective, or send them to a processer elsewhere to extract the two precious seeds (beans) per cherry.

There are millions of coffee farmers and billions of people around the world who rely on coffee to start or ease their day. Between them, green coffee traders are involved in sorting, grading, shipping, insuring, importing, exporting and distributing the unroasted beans. There are also brokers who sell the beans to roasters who build flavor through heat-treatment and ready it for further sale. Coffee can be packaged, blended, or otherwise sold to coffee companies. It also needs to be last mile transported to wherever it will be sold. Finally, after all these steps, people buy the coffee and take it home to brew.[20]

With each of these transactions – and especially in the later steps – the price increases to the point where, per kilo, you might be paying 200 times what the coffee farmer earned. Latte-drinkers and espresso-sippers struggle to make inroads into that system because it is too big and complex to have any leverage points a regular human could access.

In certain circles, we talk and hear a lot about "THE GLOBAL FOOD SYSTEM" as if it were a monolith, when in fact it is unplanned – but not incoherent. Decentralized and dynamic, the global food system is not managed or governed by any identifiable actors or entities – but, as we will soon see, it coheres and takes its shape around the values of a neoliberal capitalist techno-industrial economy. It continues to mutate in response to factors such as economic conditions, financial speculation, technological innovation, consumer demand, weather patterns, climate pressures, regulations, and geopolitical events. It isn't the only food system we've got, but because it is a transnational, industrial behemoth that reaches across much of the spinning rock we live on, it gets the most play. It is also responsible for many of the problems that we've got to reckon with.

You might be wondering: *So what is the purpose of the current global food system?* And you might reasonably assume the answer ought to be: *to feed the world.* By taking a look at how the system is behaving and what impacts it is having, we can get a sense of its purpose. So let's return to this question in the next chapter – after we've traced how we got to the food system(s) we have today and done the now unavoidable inventory.

Food from Farms

Farming is a foundational component of most food systems. This may seem obvious: farms are where most food comes from. But not all food systems – across time and even today – are agri-food systems. Before the dawn of agriculture – a revolution that happened almost contemporaneously in several parts of the world – food was foraged. For at least 95 percent of our species' history, humans gathered, caught, trapped, and hunted for their food.[21] Then, around 12,000 years ago, around the start of the Holocene epoch and its stable, supportive climate, women began farming. They started cultivating wheat and barley in the Fertile Crescent of the Middle East and Mediterranean basin and tending the first rice paddies in China. Animals quickly became humans' companions. In Mesopotamia, pastoralism – a nomadic way of life centered around the grazing of livestock – developed alongside domestication of plantlife, and provided a broader, more stable resource base.

Thousands of years later, Merriam-Webster Dictionary tells us agriculture is the science, art, or practice of cultivating the soil, producing crops, and raising livestock and in varying degrees the preparation and marketing of the resulting products. The word "agriculture" is derived from the Latin *agricultura*, a portmanteau of *ager, agr-* "field" and *cultura*, "growing, cultivation." (Keep this connection to culture in mind.) Agriculture transformed human society, and the prospects for our species, by enabling us to actively plan for more consistent food supplies, reducing the need for nomadic or seasonal migrations, enabling settlement and the growth of civilizations, and catalyzing an exponential boom in human population. Culture, civilization and food are about as interrelated as they seem, all coming from the same root.

Early agriculture is believed to have been community-oriented and, in many ways, naturally embedded in a web of relationships. While there were, of course, differences based on what kinds of crops grew where and what kinds of methods farmers found most effective, the basic premises were similar and the associated economies were small. Farming also created surpluses allowing some people to devote their time and energy to other tasks, creating sharper divisions of labor in society. But for the most part, available land, labor, technologies, preservation and transportation methods imposed some limits on how much surplus could be created and valuably maintained.

From Agriculture to Agribusiness

Much of that changed as modernizing agricultural methods, capitalist economics, settler colonialism, and imperialism combined to drastically alter the land now known as the Americas – and eventually to change how much of the world farms and eats. During the age of exploration and conquest, Europeans brought new foods to old places – and old forms of oppression to new places. Agriculture – and invocations of its inherent virtuousness– were quickly and consistently called upon to justify appropriative land claims and the genocidal campaigns that enabled them. With a seemingly unending expanse of land to grab and farm, settlers depleted soil, exhausted plots, abandoned them, and then cleared and cultivated new areas. This was relatively easy to do when the labor was supplied by indentured servants and enslaved Africans. European settlers were swiftly embedded in transatlantic markets, for which they produced commodities (crops, especially portable and storable crops, chiefly produced to be fungible articles of commerce and objects of trade) and from which they received both in-kind goods and cash. By the late eighteenth century – a period during which U.S. agriculture featured both the yeoman small-holders of American lore and the plantation owners of American shame – the contours of agribusiness were taking shape in and shaping the United States. In fits and starts throughout a long and bellicose nineteenth century, as the American financial system formed and became more sophisticated, American farmers became increasingly embedded in a capitalist system of agricultural production and exchange. Proto-agribusiness figures bought financial instruments and focused on the production of staple crops as they pursued greater market embeddedness and attendant profits. During this period, it became possible to achieve a land-based bourgeois life-style – but doing so required the purchasing of machinery, the hiring of wage workers or the purchase (and oppression) of chattel slaves to ramp up total output.[22]

By the early twentieth century, the age of industry promised continued intensification, even after emancipation of the enslaved. Industrial agriculture took as its primary (and short-sighted) aim increasing outputs and yield in any given season. It was and remains more or less unconcerned with maintaining a healthy environment or even with the long-term quality and productivity of land in production.

Industrial agriculture also stands on the shoulders of an unlikely cousin – war. Violent conflict has long shaped the ways in which we grow and consume food. In the modern era, we have seen the technologies of war become the technologies of agriculture. The world wars of the early twentieth century spurred the synthesis of chemical compounds intended to maximize harm and hasten victory. In peacetime, the developers of these compounds and associated technologies created markets for their products in other industries – including agriculture. There, they became effective pesticides, herbicides, and synthetic fertilizers, credited with maximizing agricultural productivity during what we now call the Green Revolution. Converting atmospheric nitrogen via the Haber-Bosch method produced wildly devastating explosives beginning in WWI and today remains the cornerstone of agricultural productivity.[23] The herbicide 2,4-D – which was invented as part of the chemical boom of World War II and used in the defoliant Agent Orange sprayed across Vietnam – has been widely used as an agricultural herbicide, very unsafely,[24] since the 1940s.[25] Most recently, the unmanned aerial vehicle (drone) and sensor technologies accelerated for use in the more recent wars in Iraq and Afghanistan are increasingly being introduced into very large scale industrial farming and ranching operations for soil and field analysis, crop spraying and monitoring, and irrigation.[26]

After more than a century of intensive industrialization and biotechnification, agriculture has been subsumed by agribusiness. According to a proud post by an agribusiness group:

> As culture has evolved, farming has become more than merely an in-house method of survival. It has become a thriving industry for business development and technological advancement. As new tools are established and research is conducted, every single factor of agriculture is being transformed into what we now call agribusiness. The supply chain has developed into a global industry that allows farmers to focus their work on growing their crops more efficiently and precisely. Production is made easier with the help of companies that produce farming machinery, supply seeds and develop technological tools to help farmers make precise decisions when planting and harvesting. These companies create an ecosystem that turns agriculture into agribusiness.[27]

To be clear, they are chuffed about this. They view this state of affairs as a triumph *because* they use neither nature nor wellbeing as their measure.[28] This is part of why we take issue with it. This agribusiness model works because it has been allowed to ignore, push off, and escape responsibility for all kinds of harms – the so-called "negative externalities" of industrial agriculture and agribusiness. Further, the idea of agri-business as an "ecosystem" does not pass our laugh test. Ecosystems consist of a biological (living) community that occurs in a particular locale, the physical and chemical factors that make up its abiotic (non-living) environs, and the relationships among and between organisms and their environment. The "externalities" of agribusiness have eroded and poisoned countless ecosystems and caused the demise of life within them.

Examining Those "Externalities"

Without a doubt, the global industrial food system delivers calories with vigor. For certain favored crops, under select climatic conditions, and in the absence of disruptions, industrial agriculture does indeed have higher yield per hectare than other production methods. But, is it really all that stands between humanity and a future of mass starvation due to population growth running ahead of food production? How much of that "food" actually feeds humans versus livestock versus internal combustion engines (as biofuels)? And how does it impact our relationships with ourselves, each other, our communities, and our planet? Let's take a closer – but still pretty quick – look.

Environmental Impacts

Land Use: At present, 75 percent of the Earth's land and 66 percent of the marine environment have been significantly altered by human actions.[29] Most of this change has been associated with agricultural production and livestock grazing, which are by far the most extensive human uses of land globally.[30] The amount of land used for agriculture increased nearly sixfold in just a few centuries, between 1700 and 1980.[31] Livestock grazing takes up 26 percent of the planet's ice-free land. (Much of this grazing land isn't suited for crop production; well-managed grazing can be a good thing as livestock convert grasses that humans cannot eat into meat and milk that we can.[32]) Yet, not all cropland is being used to produce actual food for humans: 33 percent is used to produce feed for livestock.[33] On top of this, another four percent of the world's agricultural land (and about four percent of its fresh water are now used for growing biofuels). About one-third of the world's malnourished population could be fed by using resources now used for biofuel production.[34]

Nevertheless, so much land is used to produce feed and fuel because these uses make more money.

Agrarian writer Wendell Berry reminds us that "the true measure of agriculture is not the sophistication of its equipment, the size of its income, or even the statistics of its productivity but the good health of the land." As we will see, the health of land used for agriculture is in critical condition.

Deforestation: Industrial agriculture is driving 75 percent of global tropical deforestation.[35] Deforestation contributes more carbon pollution to the atmosphere than all the world's cars, trucks, ships, trains, and airplanes combined.[36] Cattle farming is currently directly responsible for 71 percent of Latin American deforestation, making it the single largest driver of deforestation across the region.[37] Across the tropics, between 1980 and 2000, "over 55 percent of new agricultural land came at the expense of intact forests and 28 percent came from disturbed forests."[38] Within the logics of the global food system, forests are worth more dead than alive. This is because deforestation offers a one-two profit punch: first, fast profits can be made from the extracted forest products; then, after clearing, easy profits can be made from producing vast monocultures of soy and corn. Relatively poor people who live in the Global South are the ones actually felling the trees and tilling what remains, but the primary drivers of rainforest destruction come from other parts of the world in the form of demand for cheap forest products and cheap meat. Heedless of the consequences, powerful actors in the global food system are effectively skinning our planet alive, without noticing or caring that the Earth, like the worms who dwell in its crust, breathes through its skin.

Soil: As humans clear and till land, soils that take hundreds of years to build are lost. "Currently, 80 percent of the world's agricultural land suffers moderate to severe erosion, while 10 percent experiences slight erosion.... As a result of soil erosion, during the last 40 years about 30 percent of the world's cropland has become unproductive."[39] We lose about 10 million hectares of cropland each year due to soil erosion based on our farming practices. We are losing soil somewhere between 10 and 40 times faster than we are renewing it, which leaves us a future of food insecurity.[40]

Soil organic matter levels are also falling in agricultural and deforested lands. Soils rich in organic matter are better able to retain water and nutrients and host more complex fungal ecologies, all of which makes plants, whether wild or agricultural, thrive. Healthy levels of organic matter also improves soil structure, reduces erosion, and improves quality in both groundwater and surface waters. Declines in soil biodiversity decrease the nutritional quality of food crops, with disproportionate impacts on subsistence farming communities vulnerable to micronutrient deficiency.[41]

Soil loss is a bad thing for both the prospects of future food production and the climate crisis. Healthy soils store about three times the amount of carbon that is stored in living plants and twice the carbon stored in the atmosphere. Undisturbed soils can also store carbon for centuries.[42]

Water Consumption: Agriculture accounts for the largest human consumptive use of water. In a world that climate change is rapidly making more arid, fresh water is going to be one of our limiting resources. In many regions, it already is.[43] Agriculture accounts for about 70 percent of the groundwater pumped for human use globally and about 53 percent of the groundwater pumped in the United States.[44] Often, and especially in agricultural areas dependent upon groundwater-fed irrigation, water is being pumped at a faster rate than natural processes can recharge underground aquifers. In many places, groundwater depletion is so severe that "well yields have decreased, pumping costs have risen, water quality has deteriorated, aquatic ecosystems have been damaged, and land has irreversibly subsided."[45] Excessive groundwater depletion affects major regions of North Africa, the Middle East, South and Central Asia, North China, North America, and Australia, as well as some other localized areas throughout the world. A parched planet cannot support food production or people. We need both food and water to survive.

Water Pollution: Agriculture doesn't just use water, it also pollutes water. As water, in the form of rainfall or irrigation, runs off agricultural land it carries fertilizers (principally, nitrogen and phosphorus), pesticides, and sediment into waterways introducing excessive nutrients, toxic substances, and sedimentation that disturb aquatic ecologies and can lead to localized dead zones. Typically, just half of the nitrogen-based fertilizers applied are actually taken up by plants, leaving lots of mobile nitrogen, which can be lost as nitrate to groundwater or as the gasses nitrous oxide (a potent greenhouse gas), dinitrogen, or ammonia to the atmosphere. Additionally, synthetic pesticides contaminate air and water, creating acutely toxic conditions in agricultural areas and traveling through the food supply as residues on all kinds of foods – especially the whole, fresh produce that is supposed to be the most health-giving.[46] Unable to escape runoff, marine creatures are also imperiled by the injudiciously applied chemicals that flow out of agri-business and into delicate wetlands and waterways.[47]

Wild Biodiversity Loss: Species extinction is happening at rates 1,000 to 10,000 times higher than the natural background extinction rate – at either end of that spectrum, it's bad. Agriculture and fisheries are driving incredible impacts to biodiversity loss on land and sea. Researchers determined that some 5,407 species (62 percent) on the "red list" of threatened species were threatened by agriculture alone – not necessarily by other factors like overexploitation, urban development, invasion and disease, pollution, or transport and energy production.[48] The extinction of wild pollinators such as bees, butterflies, and bats ought to be of particular concern – without them annual global crop output is expected to decrease by \$235–577 billion.[49] These losses will not be isolated to particular regions or food types: more than 75 percent of global food crops—including fruits, vegetables, and some of the most valuable crops such as coffee and cocoa—rely on pollinators.[50] Industrial production and harvesting systems take their toll on a species which support production, including pollinators, predators, fungi, aquatic organisms, and soil biota.[51] In industrial agriculture, pollinators are synergistically and negatively impacted by a range of factors, including pests, pathogens, pesticides and poor nutrition. Holistic entomologist Nissa Coit explains that "exposure to chemical pesticides and a uniform diet of monoculture flowers reduces the ability of both wild and managed pollinators to fight off the infections and parasites that plague them, especially when they are forced to live in very high population densities due to habitat degradation or destruction and the hoarded hives positioned together for mass bloom events in monocultures that stretch for miles and miles." The decimation of these species is often viewed by industrial farmers and agribusiness interests, when it is thought of at all, as acceptable collateral damage in a noble fight to produce food. In reality, it is self-defeating and has disastrous implications well beyond their farms or sectors.

Agrobiodiversity: Industrial agriculture evinces both reckless disregard for life that is not deliberately cultivated and reckless disinterest in the variety of life forms. Three-quarters of the global food supply draws on just twelve crops and five livestock species.[52] Just four crop species – maize/corn, wheat, rice and potatoes – dominate the industrial food system. Efforts to improve and support the production of these four species suck up the majority of agricultural research investment. Indeed, nearly half of all private sector agricultural research concentrates on one single crop – maize/corn.[53] This may be the most compelling evidence of just how reductionist the industrial production system is. Presented with abundant life and abundant diversity, it favors these four crops. And then, through industrial processing, it often reduces them to white starches – the literal "white supremacy" of commodity food. In contrast to that one crop's hold on the food system, more than 8,800 livestock breeds have been recorded globally, representing a rich biodiversity at the genetic level.[54] Yet, we know that just six livestock species – chicken, cattle, sheep, ducks, goats, and pigs – dominate global production[55] (measured by both count and mass). Humans neglect agrobiodiversity at our collective peril. Farms and farming regions can not adapt to new stresses (e.g., climate volatility) unless they have high inherent resilience and adaptive capacity, which comes from high heterogeneity/ biodiversity at all levels (seeds/breeds and agroecosystems). Remember the lessons of the Irish potato famine – Irish farmers relied on a single species of potato for nearly all of their food in the nineteenth century; blight devastated the country's food supply. In other words, over-reliance on a narrow set of species or genetics, and monocultural production systems (to say nothing of "monocultures of the mind"[56]) and leave us dangerously vulnerable to future famine.[57]

It can be helpful to see losses in wild biodiversity, diminishment of agrobiodiversity, and the scale of agriculture alongside each other: Since the dawn of agriculture and civilization, human action has eliminated 83 percent of wild mammals and 50 percent of wild plant life. Now humans, who represent just 0.01 percent of all living things, along with the livestock we raise constitute an astounding 96 percent of the mammalian biomass currently on Earth.[58]

Oceans: Humans reached into the sea for sustenance long before the dawn of agriculture, and half the global human population continues to rely upon wild-caught fish for nutrition (especially protein and micronutrients), culture, and identity. Yet, most contemporary commercial fishing bears little resemblance to the small-scale, subsistence or community-centered coastal fishing of earlier eras. Industrialization of fisheries, technological advances, and the proliferation of abusive labor practices in offshore settings have made it possible to remove somewhere between 0.97 and 2.7 trillion fish from the oceans each year, not including illegal harvesting, bycatch, and discards. If your brain, like ours, struggles to make sense of such massive numbers, try this: humans remove millions fish from the oceans every minute.[59] Such prodigious extraction is accomplished with techniques that vacuum up sea life, dredge the seafloor, capture non-target species, shatter corals, uproot seaweeds, and generally destroy habitats. Though vast and home to approximately 78% of the animal biomass on this planet, the seas are not inexhaustible.[60] Some projections indicate that by 2050 eighty-eight percent of fish stocks will be either overfished or below their target biomass.[61] Little is left for the creatures that live in the sea or to nourish hundreds of millions of the world's poorest coastal people.[62]

Healthy, living oceans are also essential to a stable, life supporting climate. Marine photosynthesizers like phytoplankton and seaweed produce large quantities of oxygen and oceans act as powerful sinks for both carbon dioxide and heat. But the oceans are imperiled by agricultural and food system activity, which contributes to large dead zones, millions of tons of plastic pollution (e.g., the single use packaging our groceries come in), and aggressive overfishing that throws marine food webs out of balance. While quite different from each other, terrestrial and marine ecosystems – and the living beings that make their homes in each – are interconnected and interdependent. In the oft-quoted words of oceanographer Sylvia Earle, "No water, no life. No blue, no green."

Waste: At least 31 percent of food that is grown, shipped or sold globally is lost or wasted. This means that all the bad stuff you just read about happens in service of producing, processing, or transporting food that never nourishes anyone. When food rots in landfills, not only are the nutrients, energy, resources, and labor that went into creating it wasted, but the uncontrolled decomposition process releases methane, a greenhouse gas that is 80x worse for the climate than CO_2 emissions in the first 20 years after it enters the atmosphere. Food waste occurs all along the food supply chain. It happens on farms where a crop might not be harvested if it has cosmetic blemishes or falls out of specifications for processing, if labor is too expensive or in short supply, or if there isn't a ready and willing market. Less frequently, it also happens in processing, when residuals can't be directed to a higher and better use. At the retail level, waste occurs when grocers throw out bananas that are turning brown or fill a dumpster with unopened product past its best-by date, which is typically an indicator of optimal taste or texture, not safety. In restaurants, waste occurs in kitchens when convenience, efficiency, and appearance overshadow creative use and reuse of ingredients and in dining rooms when folks eat less than they've ordered, don't take the excess home, or bring it home but let it molder in the fridge. We waste 17 percent of the food that makes it to retail settings, restaurants, or households worldwide. Food wasted accounts for 8–10 percent of global greenhouse gas emissions.[63]

Speaking of leftovers, we've got to get real about one of the biggest sources of food waste, especially in wealthier nations: all of us. In the U.S., households are the number one contributor to food in landfills, responsible collectively for 37 percent of what is an almost entirely avoidable 52 million-ton methane-making mess.[64] Let's make this personal: on average, every American sends over 200 pounds of food waste – much of it still edible, still food – to landfills. Few of us are aware of how each tin of uneaten take-out and refrigerator cleaning days add up. Even fewer realize that we can actually do better by the climate, environment, laborers, and our own wallets simply by eating more of what we buy and responsibly redirecting any unavoidable excess back into the food system through some combination of sharing what's still good, gathering it to be used as animal feed, or composting.

Climate: Globally, the food system contributes approximately 34 percent of greenhouse gas emissions through deforestation and land use, agricultural production and processing, plastics and aluminum packaging, long-distance transport and food waste. Over 70 percent of those emissions come directly from agriculture, forestry and land use – a combination of deforestation, soil degradation, fertilizer production and application, enteric fermentation from livestock, among other related factors. Additionally, because materials, labor, and processing are sourced from and located wherever is least expensive (and often, least regulated), sourcing and out-sourcing can necessitate multiple instances of transcontinental and transoceanic transportation. Nearly 29 percent is attributable to middle-of-the-system activities like refrigeration, food processing, packaging, and transportation.[65]

As if that wasn't staggering enough, consider this: even if humans were magically able to cease greenhouse gas emissions from all other major sources, sticking with the food system we've got, would still cause global temperature rise to exceed 1.5 degrees Celsius by the middle of the twenty-first century. Oxford University researchers concluded that "emissions from [unaltered] food systems alone would result in a world with more than 1.5C of warming by 2065, and 2C shortly after 2100."[66] To meet the 1.5C target (again, alongside a complete clean energy transition) we would need to dramatically change our system from the way food is grown, by whom, how it gets to us, and even what we eat. Plainly, the climate will not allow humans to survive the ways we feed ourselves.[67]

As we extract resources, pollute and degrade nature, we risk exceeding the planet's boundaries and degrading the Earth's capacity to regulate environmental processes.[68] Yes, just like us, the planet has boundaries – and we ought to be respecting them just as we would respect the boundaries of people in our lives. If we don't, we can't be in right relationship with our planet. Johan Rockström and team have mapped nine planetary boundaries in the Earth system: (1) climate change, (2) biodiversity integrity (genetic and functional diversity of ecosystems and their functions); (3) ocean acidification; (4) depletion of the ozone layer; (5) atmospheric aerosol pollution; (6) biogeochemical flows of nitrogen and phosphorus; (7) freshwater use; (8) land-system change; and (9) release of novel chemicals.[69] As we violate those boundaries, we push the planet outside of what is called "the safe operating space for humanity"[70] and it gets far more difficult to maintain and improve air and water quality, build healthy soils, sequester carbon, and provide coastal protection from storms. In other words, Earth systems can only take so much of our crap – they will only put up with a certain amount of our disregard and abuse. When we violate these boundaries, the Earth will break up with us – and with many other forms of life – and it will kick us out of our only home.

Ultimately, this reduced capacity undermines the prospects for the kind of economic development that growth-oriented capitalism promises it will eventually deliver. Progress toward 35 out of 44 (80 percent) of the assessed targets of the United Nations Sustainable Development Goals related to poverty, hunger, health, water, cities, climate, oceans, and land is imperiled by breaching planetary boundaries – something the global food system has helped to hasten.[71]

There's a spot of good news in all this, though. In the ten years since the planetary boundaries framework was first articulated, scientists the world over have studied it intensively and conducted complementary research. After all that scrutiny, Johan Rockström and his team have confidently concluded that "if we can be planetary stewards of the nine planetary boundaries, we stand a good chance of a prosperous, socially inclusive future within a safe operating space on Earth." So, when we devised the principles by which we can reform the food system (introduced in Chapter Four), we made sure they were capable of addressing these boundaries, too.

Exploiting Some Humans So Others Can Eat

Exploitation extends beyond the environment. Hundreds of millions of food systems workers are chewed up and spat out by the food system at any given time. These aren't easy jobs: they involve hard and fast-paced physical labor for long hours, often in the unsheltered outdoors and in close proximity to dangerous machinery, toxic chemicals, or powerfully built animals. For this, most are paid poverty wages, and receive no medical benefits or paid sick days. These workers often have no choice but to rent space in dilapidated buildings that are crammed full of far more people than legal occupancy levels permit. They rarely have access to reliable transportation unless it is operated by their employers.[72]

Even in legal systems that recognize union rights, farmworkers and some of their food processing counterparts tend to be excluded from the laws that protect rights to collective organization, action, or bargaining. Many perform seasonal work and have few opportunities to earn wages for several months of each year; some must migrate long distances from home and family in search of temporary work on farms. Cultural and language barriers reinforce social isolation.

Food systems workers are subjected to racism, sexism, harassment, assault and unsafe working conditions at alarming rates. Worse yet, an indeterminate but not insubstantial portion of the estimated 24.9 million victims of human trafficking worldwide, including children, are forced to work in agriculture, fisheries, food processing and service. Many of these forced laborers are also victims of sexual violence.[73]

Most human labor in food systems takes place beyond the view of the eating masses. Farming, ranching, fishing and food production activities overwhelmingly occur in remote, rural regions with low population and limited tourism or take place far off-shore. Even when that labor is in the same building – a restaurant or cafeteria – much of it is obscured behind the kitchen door and, still in the U.S. today, legally compensated below minimum wage.[74] Without access to nuanced accounts of workers' lives, the imaginations of consumers – when they think of food systems workers at all – use pastoral agrarian myths, idealized notions of the noble nature of farmwork, comforting images of kitchens, and the creative aspects of cookery to construct comforting stories about opportunity to earn and upward mobility.

Human Nourishment, Health, and Wellbeing

The system producing all of the harms cataloged above has been aggressively successful at creating affordable abundance. Not real abundance, not liberatory abundance, definitely not pleasure, but illusory abundance – a calorie-profuse global food supply that routinely contains one and a half times as many calories than needed to feed everyone.[75]

A calorically profuse food supply – which is not necessarily the same as a nutritionally appropriate one – demonstrates that food insecurity is more a function of malapportionment or poor distribution of the supply rather than undersupply.[76] Even as the global human population has continued to grow, per-person food availability has more than kept pace – even with roughly half of all grain getting fed to livestock or being used for industrial purposes and agro-biofuels.[77] Food is *available* on the planet, but it cannot be reliably *accessed* or *utilized* by the poor in a stable manner.

We have the means, the technology, and even the supply to feed the world. How then, is it possible that today nearly two billion of our fellow humans do not have access to sufficient, safe, and appropriate food.[78] Of these, close to 828 million – nearly one in ten humans – experienced severe levels of food insecurity in 2022. Hunger amid global sufficiency is unacceptable in all its manifestations, but it is especially unbearable and damning in the 144 million children under age 5 affected by stunting and the 47 million affected by wasting, or acute undernutrition, a condition caused by limited nutrient intake and infection. Inadequate nourishment in the first 1,000 days is known to cause irreversible brain damage and lifelong chronic diseases and to impair a child's ability to learn and eventually earn a decent living. This makes it harder for a child to rise out of poverty and increases the chances that the next generation, if there is one, will remain food insecure.[79]

Further, at the start of this decade, the Food and Agriculture Organization of the United Nations projected that the number of people affected by hunger would surpass 840 million by the turn of the next decade. In other words, before and without accounting for the pandemic, the global governance body charged with addressing global hunger predicted it would spread unchecked – and just three years into the 2020s, we're nearly there. In December 2020, the World Food Programme warned that the number of people "marching towards starvation," (i.e., suffering from acute starvation) had leapt from 135 million to 270 million – a terrifying 82 percent increase during a global health crisis.[80] In the 2022 edition of *The State of Food Security and Nutrition in the World* report, the UN not only catalogued the sharp rises in hunger and the obstacles to accessing a healthy and sufficient diet faced by billions throughout the pandemic and into the economic trough that has followed, but it also predicted that global hunger will persist through the remainder of this decade. "Looking forward, projections are that nearly 670 million people (8% of the world population) will still be facing hunger in 2030 – even if a global economic recovery is taken into consideration." Such staggering levels of hunger and the widespread ill-health that results from poor nutrition are overwhelming evidence of an agrifood economy that is better at producing profits than it is at allocating food resources equitably. Education, opportunity, and economic progress all suffer in the context of this massive misallocation.

At the same time, and in the same global food system, diet-related disease impacts low and middle income countries disproportionately, which at this point cannot come as a surprise.[81] What is surprising is that being a rich country is not hunger-preventive either. For example, "the UK had the third cheapest basket of food in the developed world, but also had the highest food poverty in Europe in terms of people being able to afford a healthy diet."[82] And, to further prove that we are on the right track to take things into the *agrelational* world, the authors of that report recommended agroecological farming for human and planetary health – a decidedly relational approach.[83] Since we are coining a phrase here, *agrelational food systems are those that place people, land, and climate above profit.* In contrast to agribusiness, which is relentlessly reductionist, optimizing, and single-minded, *agrelationship* is nuanced, balancing, and mutualistic.

Modeled and Manufactured Food Supply Fears

Despite the profusion of cheap, fungible foodstuffs, many elite experts and power brokers in the food system clamor about calamitous food shortages. Using the Global Agriculture Perspectives System (GAPS) modeling methodology, the Food and Agriculture Organization of the United Nations (FAO) projects that we need to produce "60 percent more food needed by 2050."[84] These alarming predictions of scarcity are a gift to the titans of agri-business, who propound that they – and only they – can prevent looming shortage and that they – and only they – operate at a scale sufficient to a task of this scope and significance.

They also happen to be wrong.

Global food supply modeling is tricky business. Such models need to integrate biophysical, social, economic, and institutional components and make assumptions about future conditions. (It's not something we'd ever attempt – and perhaps the complexity indicates that attempts to understand food systems at smaller-than-global geographical scales makes more sense.) Yet, as bioscientist Jonathan R. Latham has amply demonstrated, the GAPS model makes some glaring and avoidable mistakes that cause it to either underestimate present and future global food supply or to overestimate global food demand now and at midcentury.[85] Among other flaws, GAPS assumes that current agricultural production systems are optimized for productivity, when in fact many are instead designed to optimize profits or to easily gain access to government subsidies. It also erroneously assumes that global food production is approximately equal to global food consumption each year, but we know that a significant amount of annual global food production winds up in storage, where it degrades and is disposed of without ever being counted by GAPS – or being put to the purpose of feeding those who are actually malnourished in the present. Latham concludes and we agree: "There is no global shortage of food. Even under any plausible future population scenario or potential increases in wealth, the current global glut will not disappear due to elevated demand."[86]

That said, climate chaos, conflict, social unrest, and warfare will almost certainly mess with both supply and demand in ways that are particularly difficult to model and pose real challenges to future food security and sufficiency. An all too real example of this is unfolding presently. As war rages in Ukraine, one of the world's breadbaskets, farmers are displaced and shipments via the Black Sea are interrupted.[87]

But beware of the single-solution peddlers – agrochemical companies that masquerade as seed sellers, equipment suppliers who have thrown in with surveillance technologists. They catastrophize GAPS predictions for the purpose of presenting their proprietary "sustainable intensification" strategies as our only hope. They'd have us all believe that intensive application of synthetic pesticides and heavier reliance on genetically modified or edited crops grown in bigger monocultures are the best way to boost food production. This is a classic case of letting the wolf guard the hen house. Promoting "sustainable intensification" to address an illusory food crisis will only intensify the climate and environmental conditions that pose the most imminent threats to a sufficient and secure food supply.[88]

Bigger Isn't Better, but Is Small Sufficient?

When she talks about the problems of giantism in agriculture and conglomeration in the food system, Nicole often gets asked: *Well, what is the right size for a farm?* This question shows she's convinced the asker that bigger isn't necessarily better. But it also reveals that they haven't yet understood this, too, as a question of relationship. Appropriate scale isn't an objective truth or a one-size-fits-all proposition. It's a matter of matching the right acreage, light infrastructure, and appropriate, ideally open-source technologies with land, climate, labor. It is also about what is being grown or raised and what management practices are being used. While it would be convenient to cheerily answer "five acres!" such a response could only be rooted in the reductive logic that messed up farming in the first place. Fifteen acres of biointensive horticulture with season-extending greenhouses and 100 acres of mixed ruminants munching on pasture grasses and resting beneath the shade of fruit and nut trees both fit within an agrelational food system.

A smaller farm future offers an appealing alternative to the current industrial farm fallacy. Small farms are already making major contributions to local and global food supplies. Cargill makes dubious and exaggerated claims about its role in "nourishing the world." While it, the world's largest privately held company, is busy bulldozing ancient ecosystems and suborning child labor – small scale farmers are serving as the main agricultural producers in many nations, especially those with developing economies. More than two billion people across the world depend on 500 million smallholder farms (less than 2 hectares in size) for their livelihoods. Solid figures on just how much of the total global food supply is produced on small farms are elusive – estimates range from 70 percent at the high end[89] to around 30 percent on the low end.[90] More reliably, we believe that small farms produce about 80 percent of the food consumed in both Asia and sub-Saharan Africa. Without getting too hung up on the comparative virtues and flaws of various modeling methods, we are satisfied to simply say that a whole lot of the world isn't being nourished by the likes of Cargill, ADM, Bunge, and Dreyfus, the titans of the global grain trade. And even if that model is presently making significant contributions to global supply, there is no reason to believe it is the only, or the best, way to meet that need. Indeed, in the words of environmental economist David Fleming, "The claim that industrial agriculture is the only way of feeding a large population is about as scientific as a belief in Creationism – and far more damaging."

Social scientist Chris Smaje makes a compelling case for reorganizing society around local economies, self- and community-provisioning, agricultural diversity and a shared ethos in his book *A Small Farm Future*. He demonstrates how before the industrial era and the rise of cheap fossil energy, it was common for societies to meet their needs by using "mixed farming strategies that carefully optimized the relationships between woodlands, fields, pastures, gardens and livestock (raised primarily for the ecological work they did on the farm, not for their meat), with the farm household as the hub of these ecological flows."[91] Such societies, found the world over, weren't entirely market-based or entirely collectivist but a blend of both. How did these low-impact agrarian societies manage it? Local cooperation, collective organization, and management of commons were key.

It should come as no surprise that something like Chris Smaje's small farm future would require a far larger percentage of people to spend at least a portion of their time stewarding small landholdings near to where they live to contribute to provisioning food, fiber and other necessities. This probably wouldn't end up in the same single-family household configuration that dominates much of America's underpopulated rural regions today. Instead, we might imagine sharing households with a small group of other people and working alongside them to provision collectively. If this calls to mind the country mouse version of a co-housing community, you are on the right track. Farming and forestry are harder labor than many modern folks are accustomed to. Yet, many hands make lighter work. While a massive transition back to the land might seem far-fetched following decades of urbanization, it turns out that many people may not have much of a choice in the matter.

There. You made it through the litany of what's wrong with the global food system today. We constructed it to help you answer the question: *What is the goal of the food system?* At this point, we can probably all agree that it can't be "feeding the world" because that's just not what's happening. In the next chapter we will clarify what we think the goal is, and why we believe that goal is going to get us into much deeper trouble than we are already in, and fast. As we stay with the idea of that trouble long enough to understand and try to avert the worst of it, we may find ourselves warming to agrelationality, even if it requires more of our time, effort, and attention.

Chapter 3

Collapse and the Fall of Agricapitalism

Reassessing the Purposes of the Global Food System

A decade ago, it was *en vogue* for those of us charting a career in the then-emergent field of food systems work to talk about "broken systems," to lament their flaws, and gape at their unbelievably negative "externalities." But as some of us spent more time working within and trying to shift system dynamics, we came to see that nothing is wrong and everything is wrong at the same time. In other words, the global food system isn't broken, it is functioning as intended. It is ruthlessly effective at commodifying land, consuming lives, and feeding profits to those who already have wealth, power, and control ensuring that they keep getting more of the same. By intention and design, it extracts value from the natural world and from the bodies of a lower subjugated class of laborers. It then converts that which has been extracted into cheap calories and profits.

The purported purpose of the global food system may be to "feed the world," but now that we've briefly reviewed its impacts, it sure seems like its actual priorities are efficiency, cost minimization, market success, profit, and growth. All short-term boons that come at too high a price. With agribusiness and industrial efficiency as its cultural touchstones, maximizing production for profit as its motivation, extraction as its *modus operandi*, and conglomeration as its form, the contemporary global food system is best described as a late-stage neoliberal agricapitalist food system or what we will call *agricapitalism*.

What comes to mind when you read the word "capitalism" printed on the page? If you are like most, your brain will quickly substitute "markets and trade." But this is too simplistic a heuristic. As economic anthropologist Jason Hickel demonstrates in his book *Less Is More*, markets and trade existed for many thousands of years before capitalism and were, in and of themselves, pretty harmless. Instead, Hickel and others identify the distinguishing feature of capitalism as its organization around and dependence upon growth – and growth for the purpose of accumulation. "It is the first and only economic system in human history that requires constant expansion, at an exponential rate. The goal of capitalist growth is not to satisfy specific human needs. The goal is to generate and accumulate more capital every year than in the previous year, which requires the constant search for new 'borders' and their exceeding." Perpetual expansion, in turn, requires the ever-increasing production of commodified goods, especially but not only foodstuffs. This mechanism of reproduction became all too familiar in 2020. It is the way of a virus.

Any growth-obsessed system that rose to dominate the global economy would be disastrous for planetary wellbeing and many non-human lifeforms. At a tender age, climate activist Greta Thunberg put it plainly when she began speaking about the "fairytale of eternal economic growth" on a finite planet. She understood that it simply isn't possible to take endlessly without giving back. It is a bit curious that leading economists didn't cotton onto this common-sense contradiction much before a child did. Perhaps because she was born at a time when the artificial dualism between humans and nature – a notion that's been with us for several centuries – had begun to breakdown. But the grown-ups were likely a bit blinded by the fact that, at least between the late nineteenth and twentieth centuries in the hegemony-producing Global North, capitalism did raise standards of living, which encouraged forgiveness of its flaws.

So, how did we come to live under transnational capitalism? How did we wind up in an insatiable economic order? Not by accident. The origin story of capitalism[92] boils down to a campaign by elites to appropriate the labor of the masses so they could work less or not really at all and still accumulate wealth from its one true source: nature. To pull this off, they had to restrict people's access to commons and locally interdependent subsistence and make wage labor the only way to survive. Once that was accomplished, the task turned to suppressing the costs associated with extraction – cheapening exerts pressure to depress wages and resist environmental protections, often by ensuring that the interests of capital are better represented in the halls of government than the interests of people or planet. This is, of course, in tension with the inspiring principles of democracy. Little wonder that this system co-produces inequality and ecological breakdown.

Unless constrained by good governance – strong laws that impose limits on the exploitative methods by which profit is most easily generated, as well as laws that protect the working classes – the economic system's logic and imperatives seep deep into our psyches. Once there, they whisper: *You know, you could be rich, too.* By dangling that possibility – however unlikely – the game prevents its losers from objecting to the rules of play. Provocative anthropologist David Graeber argued in his book *Debt: The First 5,000 Years* that "financial imperatives constantly try to reduce us all, despite ourselves, to the equivalent of pillagers, eyeing the world simply for what can be turned into money – and then tell us that it's only those who are willing to see the world as pillagers who deserve access to the resources required to pursue anything in life other than money."

While its growth and frontier-seeking attributes preclude capitalism, all on its own, from being infinitely environmentally sustainable, things didn't have to get so bad so fast. The rate at which it drove us to the brink was accelerated by its pals extractivism (all take and no give) and neoliberalism (which we'll explore in a moment). It is unfair to pin the whole crime on capitalism, as it has always traveled with a rotating band of co-conspirators. Systems of socio-economic organization such as patriarchy, settler-colonialism, and chattel slavery, are among the accomplices that sharpened the blades, picked the locks, tied up the victims, and greased the wheels. Each of these bad guys used the same dualistic splitting and sorting to justify subjugating a group deemed closer to nature than those in power. Women because of their procreative potential, indigenous peoples with societies and cultures that intrinsically value the more-than-human world, and darker skinned peoples conveniently considered less evolved were all cast as closer to nature and, therefore, appropriate to dominate. With the prospect of fabulous wealth – to a degree that one's ancestors could never have imagined – in reach and ideologies-that-other in the ether, it was easy to underplay the now-obvious wrongs of subjugating women, violently displacing indigenous peoples, and enslaving other humans intergenerationally.

After "new" lands to colonize were all grabbed up and slavery abolished, capitalism needed a new pal to help with growth-promoting. It found a fitting friend in industrialism, which reductively re-organized human life around mechanization, standardization, and process optimization. In the early industrial era, the Earth was still brimming with "resources" to extract and "sinks" – clean air and clean water – into which wastes could be pumped and absorbed. The rich got richer faster, growing their enterprises into continent and globe-spanning forces that literally reshaped the landscapes of the Earth and the mind. This is the story behind the Gilded Age in America – a brief period in which it really was possible for a few families to catapult themselves into the ranks of the super-rich.

It lasted only a little while. A little under a century ago, the upper classes flew too close to the sun, and the immaterial markets in which they multiplied their wealth came crashing down. Around the same time, the extracted heart of North America cried out from the pain of plowing up nearly all its ancient tall grass prairies to make room for a bigger brand of agriculture that is still with us today. As ecological balances were obliterated, the black blizzards of the Dust Bowl rolled across the continent, blotting out the daylight and revealing that humans had accumulated and unknowingly wielded the kind of power previously believed to be reserved for god(s).

In the grip of the Great Depression that followed, it became clear that markets could not always be counted on to sort it all out – especially when wealth inequality widened to a point where the economy produced more than could be consumed by the working masses who didn't have enough income. In other words, there were, in fact, limits to how much labor could be exploited and depressed before the whole of the macroeconomy tips over. The Depression, therefore, made a plain case for some regulation to protect laborers and the environment, or at least soils. It also set the stage for the New Deal era creation of safety net programs which were designed to ensure that poverty and hunger didn't stay at such apparent and alarming levels. To return a nation with breadlines knee deep in wheat to a more sustainable, less shameful state, what now sounds like a very progressive agenda was advanced.

Witnessing the market collapse of the Great Depression and ecological crisis of the Dust Bowl in tandem made a strong impression – quite obviously, people needed some protections to survive and maybe even thrive. It looked like the responsibility to take care and make care would have to sit with the state – not the market, after all. In writing *The Great Transformation* in 1944, scholar Karl Polanyi prophesied, "To allow the market mechanism to be sole director of the fate of human beings and their natural environment... would result in the demolition of society." How right he was and how ignored he would be.

Polanyi believed we were safe from such a travesty because, at that time, he was witnessing a transformational development: the economic system had ceased to lay down the law to society and the primacy of society over economy appeared to have been secured. But from our present vantage point, we all know it did not work out that way. If, in 1945, you'd described the world we live in now and the "standard neo-liberal toolkit"[93] that it runs by, people would have gaped at you open-mouthed and confounded. Political scientist Susan George puts us back in the mind of the time: "The idea that the market should be allowed to make major social and political decisions; the idea that the State should voluntarily reduce its role in the economy, or that corporations should be given total freedom, that trade unions should be curbed and citizens given much less rather than more social protection – such ideas were utterly foreign to the spirit of the time. Even if someone actually agreed with these ideas, he or she would have hesitated to take such a position in public and would have had a hard time finding an audience."[94]

But then what happened was a horrific but very smart move by neoliberals who understood better than most that ideas and culture have power. They understood what philosopher Antonio Gramsci did, namely that societal inequality and dominance is maintained by manipulating culture including beliefs, explanations on how and why things are as they are, mores, and values. By changing culture, they could return the worldview of the ruling class to its position as the accepted norm. (The same powerful understanding also allowed misogyny, White Supremacy, and all of the isms we will address shortly to flourish when they should have quickly floundered, too.)

Desirous of a return to easy profits and rapid wealth creation and aware that transformations come from changing the goals and the culture of a system, economist Friedrich von Hayek and his students at the University of Chicago, including the now infamous Milton Friedman, got to the work of whispering a new notion: raw competition. To increase the virulence of their ideas, they not only published in scholarly literature and the popular press, but they also stood up foundations, deployed public relations strategists, and cozied up to congressmen. They stuck with the project without flagging for decades. Eventually, as this idea went viral, it created new goals, ways of looking at the world, and culture. Indeed, it may have been the primary accelerant of agricapitalism and the economic, political, and ecological disasters it has helped to advance – the very crises we're all grappling with today.

So what is the neoliberal set of values? This now-hegemonic culture that breaks instead of bridges? This idea that set us on the path that we wrote this book to address? Environmental writer George Monbiot sums it handily:

Neoliberalism sees competition as the defining characteristic of human relations. It redefines citizens as consumers, whose democratic choices are best exercised by buying and selling, a process that rewards merit and punishes inefficiency. It maintains that "the market" delivers benefits that could never be achieved by planning.

Attempts to limit competition are treated as inimical to liberty. Tax and regulation should be minimised, public services should be privatised. The organisation of labour and collective bargaining by trade unions are portrayed as market distortions that impede the formation of a natural hierarchy of winners and losers. Inequality is recast as virtuous: a reward for utility and a generator of wealth, which trickles down to enrich everyone. Efforts to create a more equal society are both counterproductive and morally corrosive. The market ensures that everyone gets what they deserve.[95]

Neoliberalism sets up winners and losers, and the losers lose big so the winners can have more. More than they need, more than they could possibly use, and more than the Earth can support.

Most of us are the losers, who deserve what we get in a system where competition is all, and success is defined as taking what you want from others, if you can possibly pull it off.

The Earth and its other inhabitants are eliminated entirely from consideration.

Climate justice writer and activist Naomi Klein identifies destruction of our relational capacity as neoliberalism's "single most damaging legacy," noting that its "bleak vision has isolated us enough from one another that it became possible to convince us that we are not just incapable of self-preservation but fundamentally not worth saving."[96] What could be further from the truth? Of course, we are worth saving. Our world is worth saving.

At its core, neo-liberalism insists that the economy should dictate its values and measures of success to society, not the other way around. When this happens, things like democracy, justice, care, equity, and even survival get in the way of the project. Probably not the arrangement we actually want. Imagine what might happen if we flipped this around and tried to create what economist Mariana Mazzucato calls a "mission economy" by first asking what kind of markets we want, rather than just going right to the question of what problems in the market need to be fixed.[97]

If we want to get out from under these pernicious neoliberal lies, we need to start shaping change in economic and food systems. We must revive the culture of agriculture, which requires releasing it from the clutches of agricapitalism. In the next chapter we will go deep into systems change so for now, here is the quickie version. We need to point out to each other the failures and problems with the old paradigm; in this case, it is the current paradigm of neoliberal capitalism. Next, we need to create and operate with flamboyant visibility from the new paradigm. We need to support each other and everyone we find living this new paradigm, making relationships and kin in ways we could never have expected.

Finally, we must prioritize sharing our message with folks who are receptive and refrain from worrying much about the criticism of those who benefit from the current system so much that they cannot or will entertain the possibility of transformation.

Perhaps relationships still feel a little too soft and squishy to you – especially as compared to the firm-yet-invisible hand of the markets. In that case, ask yourself, is the market providing any real choices, benefits, or even opportunities? If so, to whom? By our count, the winners seem to be a very select few:

- The top ten food & beverage processors control 90 percent of the industry.
- Despite a seemingly varied array of products on store shelves, four or fewer firms control at least 50 percent of the market for 79 percent of the groceries regularly purchased by Americans.
- Following recent mergers and acquisitions – the Dow-Dupont merger, Bayer-Monsanto buyout, and the ChemChina (Syngenta)-Sinochem asset merger – about 70 percent of the agrochemical industry is in the hands of three entities.
- As of 2016, the top ten fertilizer companies held 56 percent market share of an industry that saw $183 billion in revenue in 2014.
- The top four companies hold 67 percent market share of the seed industry, an industry that generated about 63 billion in revenue in 2020 and is expected to grow to $100 billion by 2026.
- Oddly (or perhaps predictably) Bill Gates is now the largest U.S. farmland owner holding at least 242,000 acres of mostly prime agricultural lands.[98]

As we focus on the cutting edges of agricapitalism, it is important to distinguish between small businesses, which quite typically operate under a steady-state, use-value logic (and have done so since long before capitalism), and shareholder-value maximizing corporations, whose main objectives must include expansion and surplus accumulation to keep the profits flowing. We can go back to Josh Crane and The Coffee Ride. Yes, Josh wants to make a living, he wants to have enough money to do the things he loves, including travel. However, his business plan is based around his belief that we can all do a little bit more to help the planet and each other. He employed a professional bike racer to deliver his coffee for a while, allowing her to get paid to train and at the same time lowering the carbon footprint of the business. Sure, Josh will ship you coffee, as he believes that stopping the whole worldwide shipping system is impossible. However, his employees have ridden more than 26,000 miles over the last eight and a half years. When the business does well, Josh, his employees, and his suppliers all do well and can return even more to the Earth. The result, for that one small business, is similar to the result for many small and family businesses across the world: livelihood as opposed to accumulation, community impact as opposed to extraction, and more relationship as opposed to more separation.

While we're posing questions, let's take a closer look at the market aspects of capitalism. It is also worth asking: *is the market in the agri-food sector really free?* Taking a look at the scale of subsidization pretty quickly demonstrates that the government is picking winners and losers. Though these examples are focused on the United States, you will get the picture:

In any given year, approximately $424.4 billion dollars of subsidies – inclusive of crop insurance, disaster programs, conservation programs, and commodity programs – are pumped into the American Agriculture sector.[99] From 1995 to 2020, about twenty-six percent of total subsidies – some $63.6 billion dollars' worth – went to the top one percent of farms and about 78 percent – $187.8 billion dollars' worth – to the top

10 percent.[100] During the same fifteen year period, 69 percent of farms in the United States did not collect subsidy payments.[101] To put a finer point on it: an astronomical sum of money from the public coffers lands in the pockets of a disproportionately small number of farms in the United States, and almost exclusively in the most highly mechanized, most resource-intensive, most ecologically degrading monocultures.

Most subsidies go to just five crops: wheat, cotton, corn, soybeans, and rice. By heavily subsidizing grains and legumes to serve as feed and inputs, industrially produced meat and highly processed corn and soy-based products stay cheap despite their environmental and social costs.[102]

Since subsidies are largely for industrially produced commodities and mostly go to larger, wealthier farms, it can be argued that they are solidifying the inequitable structures around land ownership and incentivizing environmentally harmful production methods. For example, the budget for environmental subsidy programs (about $4 billion) was just one-fourth the size of trade-related payments (totaling $16 billion) in 2019.[103]

Current policies benefit those already owning land, with just one example being the 2018 Market Facilitation Program (MFP) that provided subsidies to support farmers during the U.S.-China trade wars. White operators received 99.4 percent of all MFP payments, with an "overwhelming share of the funds" having gone to upper-middle-class and wealthy families.[104]

Talking about agriculture policy and subsidies can start to get really technical, really fast. Economic discourse is jargony, opaque and overwhelming, which makes the resulting policies seem practically apolitical. Indeed, we often talk about "the economy" and "the agricultural economy" as if these are autonomous forces. But agri-economic policy – including massive subsidy, insurance, price support, credit, and trade facilitation programs – are overtly political. These seemingly neutral economic policies justified by our need for food do actually pick winners and losers, maintain hierarchies, and shape how farmers tend land. They are put in place by politicians under the influence of oligopolistic multinationals – by which we mean the titans of Big Ag and Big Food – and their handsomely paid lobbyists. This is not hyperbole and it is getting worse rapidly: the food industry spent $175 million on political contributions and lobbying in the 2020 election cycle alone, a six-fold increase as compared to the 1992 cycle. Two-thirds went to Republicans who tend to protect the interests of capital by opposing pesky things like environmental protection and labor rights.[105]

Finally, it is worth noting that while the United States of America is not the only country to juice its agriculture sector with big subsidies, this option isn't as available to the leaders of less wealthy nations, which makes it far more difficult for farmers in other nations to compete in supposedly free international markets. When we cast humans as the architects and builders of our food systems (as well as of climate change or other eco-social crises), it is really important to remember that not all people have had an equal or equally free hand in the work. The power to reap the lion's share of the benefit from food systems was – and still is – in the hands of a few. If we leave the power where it is, would we have any reason to think those who control the system will reform it? Or are things likely to get worse?

Agricapitalism and Its Underpinnings
Under neoliberal capitalism, which has subsumed other forms of capitalism in America and the other countries to which we have exported it, the point of all private enterprise is to bring the highest financial return to existing wealth. Success, then, has the inexorable effect of concentrating wealth and power, which can easily be turned into political influence. Of course, this political influence undermines the actual purpose and promise

of capitalism, the efficient production and allocation of goods and services. This is what happens when pursuit of maximum wealth becomes the single toxic driver of neoliberal capitalism. As we have shown, this is exactly what has happened in the global food system – a system that is now captive to industrial agribusiness interests. It is no wonder hunger persists despite planetary plunder.

Development scholar Philip McMichael observes that the globalization of food trade, the concentration of corporate power, and the debt-for-development model of international finance and foreign investment combine to drive "accumulation by dispossession" through a combination of structural adjustment and displacement of smallholder agriculture.[106] Under the dominant current arrangement, which he calls the "corporate food regime," localized and relational farming and food provisioning activities must contend and compete with an influx of surplus commodity foods from the Global North, agro-industrial supermarkets, and foreign investments that drive up the price of land (so that capitalist firms can extract more resources and produce additional commodities). In combination, these forces constrain opportunities for small farmers everywhere, and especially in the Global South, to support themselves and meet their own basic needs. At the same time, in wealthier nations and urban regions, people have come to view themselves as consumers first.[107] They are separated from their food by long chains (or complex webs) of intermediaries who are driven by profit motives over a desire to nourish in the full sense of the word.

Let's not mince words: Neoliberal global capitalism compels people into an abusive relationship with the planet. There can be no right relationship with an economic system as voracious as capitalism as practiced by enthusiasts of this theory. Nor can there be any truly sustainable agriculture under neoliberal and extractive capitalism.

Upon reading that, the voice in your head might clamor, *But capitalism is what accelerated human development. It lifted so many people out of poverty. It is how we got all the nice things we have now and don't want to lose!* That voice is also correct. Two things can be true at the same time, and often are. Capitalism has offered some real benefits to real people – while exploiting others. The kind of capitalism we practiced as a global society before the neoliberals' "Great Transformation" was leaning into other philosophies of care, of a Great Society, of protection and even redistribution of wealth to a degree that could buoy us all up with that great old analogy that a rising tide lifts all ships.

Raj Patel and Jason W. Moore sum it up neatly: "For capitalism, what matters is that the figures entered into ledgers – to pay workers, to supply adequate food for workers, to purchase energy and raw materials – are as low as possible. Capitalism only values what it can count and it can count only dollars... this means that the whole system thrives when powerful states and capitalists can reorganise global nature, invest as little as they can, and receive as much food, work, energy and raw materials with as little disruption as possible."[108] In neoliberal and extractive capitalism, when we're only counting dollars, we're always discounting lives.

The -Isms, -Phobias, and -Archies That Underpin Agricapitalism

Hunger amidst plenty and want amidst waste are far from the only inequities associated with contemporary food systems. That agriculture is entwined with histories of dispossession and oppression is obvious to anyone who has paid even glancing attention to colonization and slavery let alone feudalism, monarchies, empires, and colonialism. But you have to look a whole lot closer to develop an awareness of the resource stealing, land grabbing, and corporate piracy that persist today. The global food system moves to the beat of economic systems set up to favor the business interests over the interests of people and communities and that actively support a multi-racial white supremacist patriarchy.

MRWaSP, or what the theorist Robin James calls the Multi-Racial White Supremacist Patriarchy is the ideology that explains why White Supremacy is not always all White.

"It is more cost-effective to include *some* formerly excluded/ abjected groups in racial/gender/sexual supremacy, because *this inclusion further reinforces both the supremacy of the hyperelites and the precarity of the most unruly groups* (those who pose the greatest threat to MRWaSP hegemony). As the always-brilliant philosopher Falguni Sheth explains, 'more and more men and women of color have been invited into the offices of White Supremacy to share in the destruction of other men and women of color who are vulnerable, disfranchised, and rapidly being eviscerated through the policies of a multi-racial white supremacy...A multiracial white supremacy is a system of power that has invited in—or exploited wherever it could— people of color in order to wage institutional, legal, political assaults on other black, brown, and poor people—at "home" and internationally.'"[109]

It sets up an "us versus them" competition – a breaking system where we are asked to be unconcerned with the lives of others so that we can oppress, use, and discard them with less emotional baggage.

Us vs. Them

Humans have come up with lots of ways to hoard power and marginalize those they want to keep it from. These evil, viral pieces of propaganda tell us we are separate, entirely self-interested entities. In the food system, these moves to break us apart support the actual goals of the system. They may even be critical to the success of the food system – not the goal we would like, but the goal of accumulation and profit. One of the things we noticed when we came up against the voices of agricapitalism as we pushed a bill through the Colorado legislature (more on that in Chapter Five) was that there was no hesitancy on the part of agricapitalists (in this case, largely commodity farmers and ag lobbyists) to say into the public record that they could not make money without the ability to oppress, underpay, abuse, neglect, and treat as expendable the workers in their employ. At first, this made our heads spin. We knew that our current agricapitalist system grew out of slavery, colonialism, disaster capitalism, and carceral systems (those related to imprisonment). But, somehow, we thought its beneficiaries would be better off keeping it under wraps. Did the folks making money off the bodies and labor of others actually feel like they should say this using their outside voices? We called Senator Jessie Danielson, who introduced the bill, after the hearing and said, "So they're just going to say the quiet parts out loud?" And she said, with the tired realism of a very progressive legislator, "Yes, they are." This is a stock argument that gets made as to why rights and protections are bad: we can't make money if you don't let us do the things you are calling exploitative. The more often we heard arguments of this kind, the clearer it became our political opponents were too fully immersed in neoliberal culture to recognize its zero-sum conditioning. Agribusiness lobbyists were quick to deploy breaking narratives and stoke fear of economic ruin among farm owners who were simultaneously getting squeezed by the giant multinational firms that dominate the markets for their products. The classic "us vs. them" rhetoric rendered many farmers insensible to other possible alliances, such as building solidarities with workers in a shared fight for fair prices sufficient to support living wages for all. There's nothing like having your worst expectations validated to make you want to push even harder for the kinds of legislation that blunt the sharpest edges of agricapitalism.

Just like a group of ravens is called a murder, the group of -isms and -phobias displayed in that hearing (plus some didn't show up there) is called a kyriarchy – the social system that keeps many intersecting oppressions in place.[110] Kyriarchal structures work together to characterize the connections in and distort the data about food systems. These deliberate skews and manufactured biases set many in the system against the very solutions we need to survive. Just like fear and resentment can make us lie to ourselves, greed and the addiction to surplus can make individuals and institutions deceive society in service of their own accumulation.

There are other excellent volumes devoted to unpacking the -isms, -phobias, and other socially constructed memes of manipulation that deserve your attention. We know we cannot do the thought within them justice in these pages, but we also know we must bring some of these oppressive forces to the fore so that we can keep an eye out for their insidious presence as we build relationship and seek liberation.

Colonialism

Colonialism is multifaceted domination – some combination of territorial, legal, cultural, linguistic, political, epistemic and/or economic domination – of one or more groups of people by a foreign power over an extended period of time. Seizing indigenous lands, privatizing and portioning it out to westward migrating settlers, pressing prairies and other diverse ecosystems into narrow types of production, converting land to capital, and supporting it all with a nationwide research university apparatus charged with optimizing the economic outputs of agriculture are all obvious ways that colonialism, imperialism, and agricaptialism are entwined in the United States of America. The way activist and author Patty Krawec talks about colonialism lays its anti-relational nature bare: "Colonialism works in all of us to destroy and replace: destroying relationships and replacing them with isolated identities we can move around the country. It tells us to be one thing or another and never gives any of us time to be at home with ourselves. It tells us to be ourselves but then clearly lets us know which selves are welcome and which selves are not. Whatever we are is not enough, so we grasp for something else, as if that will imbue us with meaning. And it's empty because it isn't truly ours."[111]

Racism and White Supremacy

It is impossible to read the history of agricultural workers in the United States, and elsewhere in the world, without recognizing that today's exploitative practices were originally created, enforced, and eventually cemented through legislation to systematically and durably advantage one racial group (White Europeans) over other groups (first Black Americans, then successive waves of immigrants, and today, largely Latinx people). The intergenerational economic advantages that centuries of chattel slavery, racialized and exclusionary agricultural labor laws (in most states), and a history of well-documented and widespread discrimination at the USDA are a still-living and proudly displayed legacy of colonialism and slavery in this country. Agricultural workers, alongside domestic laborers, were deliberately carved out of laws designed to protect all other workers, guarantee minimum wages and reasonable working hours, and enable collective action and power building.

Attorney and inequality expert Heather McGhee explains that both the wide span of the U.S. economy and its agricultural sector have long "depended on systems of exploitation—on literally taking land and labor from racialized others to enrich white colonizers and slaveholders. This made it easy for the powerful to sell the idea that the inverse was also true: that liberation or justice for people of color would necessarily require taking something away from white people."[112] Until we unlearn the inverse inference and disabuse ourselves of the notion that everything from farmland access to food security are a zero-sum game, racial agricapitalism will continue to stunt any justice we might hope to grow.

Sexism, Heteropatriarchy, and Gender

Nothing screams sexism like tasks demeaned when one gender is responsible for them becoming laudable when the other group takes them over. Women cook at home, men are chefs, and everyone else is left out of the neat binary of sexism. Many theorists go on about this for entire books,[113] which we can boil down to this: follow the money. Gender roles and their oppressive and limiting force on our cultures will be very clear when you see who gets paid to do what and how much they are paid for it. Entirely devaluing – not paying for – the messy, ceaseless work of domestic caretaking, including making meals day in and day out, is one way that capitalism cooks its books. If women across the world were actually paid minimum wage for the cooking, cleaning, and caretaking work they do at home, the wages would have totaled $10,900,000,000,000.00 in 2019. Yes, that's $10.9 trillion dollars (in case you had trouble with all those zeros) – and it is also more than the 50 largest companies in the world combined made around the same time.[114] Capitalism relies on heteropatriarchy to disappear the essential carework that enables all other production.

Classism and Food Deserts

Extractive capitalism and class-based society go hand-in-hand. This destructive pairing persists in food systems across time and cultures. In the twenty-first century, we have food deserts and swamps,[115] evocative metaphorical terms that make biome-loving ecologists bristle. When these conditions are racialized, as they often are, they are known as food apartheid zones.[116] These are neighborhoods, urban or rural, without ready access to fresh food and sometimes with lots of fast, highly processed food. In the U.S., these result from the redlining of both mortgages and insurance, fast food profiteering and poverty wages (targeting the underclasses and BIPOC communities), local land use, development, and zoning policies, economic opportunity, poverty wages, structural racism, and all its concomitant disparities.[117] When trying to understand the intersections of class and food environments, ground-truthing is especially important. Merely measuring the distance to the nearest supermarket or counting restaurants and retailers does not account for the lived experiences of people in the neighborhood who may not have a car, reliable childcare, or adequate time outside of multiple jobs. Such factors make grocery shopping far more arduous than quantitative measures can capture.

At the same time, the pursuit of "good food" – whether gourmet or organic – also lets those of us in the middle ease our crackling anxieties about class and status. Food and cultural studies researcher Margot Finn convincingly demonstrates that the recent good food revolution simultaneously stigmatized the foods and bodies associated with the lower class and encouraged the middle- and upper-middle classes to understand their dietary choices as a way to demonstrate that they "deserve" their status. In this context, many efforts to persuade other people to eat foods coded as "better" may even be a form of bigotry in disguise that deepens social divides.[118] In other words, class anxiety may even have us using food – a potent material for creating connection – as a wedge.

Ableism, Healthism, and Fatphobia

Healthism is the belief that there is a moral righteousness to the "healthy choices" we make around food and our bodies. It leans on ableism – the discrimination and prejudice against people with disabilities, which rooted in the belief that typical abilities are better. Healthism tills the landscape of our minds, tearing our instincts about how to nourish ourselves, destabilizing our ability to have a grateful relationship with food, and eroding our loving wonder and reverence for our bodies. It also takes a neoliberal approach to our health by situating all the factors of health in the choices of the individual. Healthism also creates a hierarchy of choices that use health as the only lens for choice. It ignores the social determinants of health, the conditions in which people are born, grow, live, work and age that shape health, as well as the influence systemic oppression that comes with race, class, gender, age, ability level, and all the other usual suspects.[119]

Our relationship to food, to the land, and to each other is always mediated by the bodies in which we live and the acculturation of those bodies. Trauma expert and redemptive healer Resmaa Menakem calls BIPOC bodies "bodies of culture," instead of bodies of color, to highlight the ways in which our relationships through and to our bodies are mediated by the culture in which we move.[120] In her book *Fearing the Black Body*, Sabrina Strings shows that idealization of thin bodies is an entwined stigma of racism, classism, and misogyny. Agricapitalism gets in on the act, too. It sneaks into our relationship with our bodies in the attention to obesity, its framing as an epidemic, and the significance attached to the Body Mass Index or BMI, a scientifically racist measure. Deeming Black and Brown bodies aberrant, deficient, or excessive, opens up opportunities for profit generation and economic growth. The diet and weight loss industry, a particularly predatory sector that intersects with the food system, seizes on this scientific racism and promotes breaking narratives that separate us from our ability to work with our bodies and our hunger intuitively. It then markets fixes for our purportedly bad bodies. But the optimization products and strategies it sells, based on the research, are about 95 percent likely to fail.

According to activist Isabel Foxen Duke, "people steadfastly cling to the belief that they can make themselves 'pure' or even immortal (outsmarting death, disease, etc.) by making 'correct' food choices—spending hours studying the literature, listening to gurus, or trying to find the golden key."[121] Agricapitalism is more than happy to produce whatever is the current golden key and sell it to us at exorbitant prices for to generate profit. The global weight loss and weight management market was valued at $192.2 billion in 2019 and projected to grow to $295.3 billion by 2027 – proving that market value and economic growth need not have a rational relationship to results or even sound science.[122] We need to separate out this diet and weight loss industry from our food system, which it has permeated, finding ways to twist our relationships to how and what we eat, and how our body feels, looks, and moves.[123]

Xenophobia and Carceralism

More than 30,000 of the people who work U.S. food production and processing jobs are actual inmates.[124] This ties the carceral system (meaning prisons and associated apparatuses) with the food systems. Additionally, many of the skilled and essential workers who are growing and picking your lettuce are treated little better than prisoners and looked down upon by their almost certainly White employers. Widespread patterns forcing people to labor on farms and in fisheries, denying them freedom of movement, and restricting their liberties are well documented by the International Labour Organization of the United Nations.[125] We also know from our experience in Colorado that some of the farm owners who employed H-2A visa workers kept them behind fences. One even insisted that the workers laboring and living on her farm wear special hats whenever they went into town, so that they would be identifiable as temporary agricultural workers – a tactic that promoted surveillance whenever they ventured off-farm.

The conceptual association of farmworkers and prisoners is further revealed in times of worker shortage. Under market theory, labor shortages should motivate employers to improve pay, benefits, and working conditions to attract workers. But such improvements, which carry expense, need not happen so long as there are other groups of people with little power and few rights who can be pressed into service and exploited instead. The agricultural sector regularly relies on structurally vulnerable guest workers and undocumented migrant workers; when these workers are under-available, farm owners turn to their elected officials[126] to facilitate access to incarcerated and formerly incarcerated people (who struggle to get better employment). Prisoners make the easiest replacements for migrants because they, too, have little ability to question conditions that put them at risk or wear down their bodies.

Historian William Horne explains how othering, exploiting and controlling show up throughout the food system and across U.S. history: "The meat-processing industry (and American foodways more broadly) run on the carceral logic of racial capitalism—the idea that bourgeois elites are superior beings who have a natural right to consume the human and nonhuman animals over whom they wield power. As with revamped systems of carcerality like the convict leasing of the Jim Crow era, these coercive forms of food production came into being in the late nineteenth century in the wake of chattel slavery in the U.S. and accompanied a renewed commitment to the genocidal removal of Indigenous nations from American landscapes. These twin acts of violence—purging the land of its inhabitants and (re)creating regimes of highly coerced agricultural labor— facilitated the mass production of industrialized exploitation across the economy. Cheap food (and thus, food work) allowed low wages in other economic sectors and in effect subsidized the broader consumer economy."[127]

These structural -isms, -phobias, and -archies are not a side effect or an inadvertent outcome of the way the food system functions. They are the methods by which agricapitalism leverages unfair advantage to achieve the goal of creating surplus for a very small number of people instead of feeding us all. Most of us – including lots of wonderful, creative, well-intentioned people working within the global food system and trying to make it better – hoped and believed that the intention was still feeding people. But we've got to face the fact that this crazy complex and totally enveloping system does not have the best interests of people or planet as the desired outcome.

Eating Injustice

Eating this much injustice does little to improve our wellbeing. And it's a lot to hold on our plates. But examining the interconnected web of oppressions that make the food system possible can also be galvanizing and motivating, at least for us. It makes us more willing to be and stay uncomfortable, to put our time, resources and our advantages on the line in ways that will actually loosen the grip of these -isms and allow power to move from where it has been tightly tethered. We hear and want to amplify the voices of those most harmed so that their experiences richly inform any kind of changes we make. As abolitionist and transformative justice activist Mariame Kaba says, "let this radicalize you rather than lead you to despair."[128]

As we've collaborated with all kinds of folks in the food system – from fifth generation dairy farmers to indigenous seed keepers, natural food marketers to food bank directors – we've noticed that the reactions to the idea of getting radical really vary. The concept of getting and being radicalized entices some and unsettles others. It's a notion that has natural resonance and broader appeal when we trace the etymology of the word. Radical comes from Latin radic-, radix, meaning "root." Its earliest uses are all about the literal roots of plants and trees; later it came to describe a fundamental component or quality of just about anything.[129] When we say "get radical" we mean, go to the root of a problem or an injustice and change what is fundamentally flawed. Roots are amazingly and inherently relational, but we rarely know it because they exist underground. Just beneath our feet, plant roots collaborate with bacteria and mycorrhizal fungi to source nutrients and water from the soil – they don't get the job done alone. Whether shallow and highly networked or tapped deep into subterranean space, roots are always sensing and adapting to their environs and the other life around them. Through her research, plant and microbial biologist Beronda Montgomery has concluded that "root responses transform soil characteristics directly and can in turn affect the physiology and ecology of all soil inhabitants." [130] Getting radical is relational and it has the potential to be transformative.

Hope, the gritty, underground kind, follows acceptance of the fact that the food system can't continue the way it is today. This isn't the kind of thing we celebrate with cupcakes and ice cream: even and maybe especially in its end-stages, the agricapitalist food system will harm the most vulnerable people just as it tried to extract the last bits of fertility and profit from the Earth and its inhabitants. However, as Michelle's grandfather used to say, "Consider the alternative." (By which he meant that any kind of being alive was better than the alternative. We mean something entirely different.) Things are already really bad – so perpetuation is not a practical or humane option. Unless the outcomes we are aiming for include even greater wealth and health disparities, more hunger amid surplus, and advancing the interests of corporations over people and planet, it's time to consider the alternative.

Collapsing Under Its Own Weight

To this point, we have painted a portrait of the agricapitalist food system for you using research and lived experience as our materials. We did this for three reasons: (1) to make the case for the necessity of a paradigm shift and the sweeping systems change that follows, (2) to help you see that "broken" parts of the system are fit-for-purpose because whatever noble aims may have once existed were subsumed by capitalism's growth imperative and profit motives; and (3) to demonstrate how all the oppressions and supremacies that thread through our society also uphold the agricapitalist orientation of the global food system.

From here on out, we take a turn towards the speculative. Theorizing what the future will bring and finding emergent examples of change that can lead us to a life-affirming future. It's not going to sound like that immediately, but we assure you that the future we describe is way better than the alternative.

What Is Collapse?

Collapse is a kind of trouble. Think of it as the kind of trouble that advances the plot of a story, cracks things open, and reveals the futility of resistance to change. Collapse slices clean through the propaganda and exposes what has really been going on all the time. The word is being uttered more frequently and openly lately, but the prospect is not new. We've had an inkling that the patterns and dynamics of humans' presence on Earth were angling in the direction of environmental and economic collapse since the publication of the book *Limits to Growth* fifty years ago, which sold 12 million copies, was translated into 37 languages, and continues to be the top-selling environmental title of all time.[131]

Collapse, at its most neutral and least terrifying, refers to processes of contraction and simplification within complex systems. This could look like a world where fuel is scarce, we use it sparingly, and we do not drive places unless it is absolutely necessary. It might mean a version of modern life where we buy and own far less stuff. Or a world in which food is way more expensive and most people only have access to staple foods. Gone are big luxuries like fine wine and imported cheese... and so are little luxuries like soda and gummy bears. And it might mean a world in which the size of the human population starts to decrease, perhaps substantially, for the first time since the fourteenth century.

It gets a little scarier when we think about chaotic varieties and phases of collapse – the kinds that are starting to unfold all around us in the early part of the twenty-first century. If you've had a nagging sense that everything seems vaguely and continually not good and certainly less promising than before, that's probably your limbic system sensing collapse.

But we still shouldn't necessarily freak out. While Hollywood has conditioned us to think of collapse as a singular, blockbuster event that brings us to the precipice of human extinction, the kind of collapse we are talking about is less meteoric and more spiralic. Collapse is what happens when societies become overly complex, dangerously deplete resources, allow gaping inequalities to form, erode social bonds, and, in our era, destabilize the life-supporting characteristics of the climate.[132]

Environmental economist David Fleming forecast a version of multi-system collapse he called a *climacteric*. He describes a twenty-first century during which a complex arrangement of dominoes tip each other over. We live with deep global deficits in energy, water, food, arable and fertile land, and rising acidified oceans (which can't provide food or store carbon). It gets worse when we begin to experience invaded ecosystems, failure of keystone species, and depleted mineral stores. The Climacteric features both a whole system thrown into chaos and concomitant resource scarcity that will make it hard to maintain infrastructure and meet human needs. It will certainly necessitate a decrease in standards of living for those in wealthy nations and make migrants of those in poorer places. The changes will increase societal pressures and, in turn, can cause economic and social fractures. We are already seeing these pressures push extreme polarization in society, cause more breaking between people, and tighten identity-based grouping. Such conditions can cause the rule of law to crumble and ideas about what justice looks like to morph into disturbing shapes (something we've also started to see in the United States). All of this interrupts the ability of education systems to hand down culture and competence. In short, "deep, interconnected, planetary tragedy."[133]

That kind of forecast isn't easy to hear, but it is based on sound data and interpretation and has been ratified by experts across a range of disciplines. (If you want to know more about collapse take a look at Shaun Chamberlin's course in EcoGather called *Surviving the Future: A Path Through Tumultuous Times*.) After reading the last chapter, which amounts to weeks of doom scrolling condensed into a few pages, collapse probably feels less speculative and nearer to us than most folks want to admit.

Here is one very concrete example that is both heartening and a little scary. We asked Josh Crane of The Coffee Ride what he saw happening in the future and he wrote us back this text:

The future is pretty uncertain. I know folks in the importing industry that are scared for the future of their jobs already. I've heard of growers having to supplement growing things like avocados because the coffee yields were too low. There's also been some work on development of some hybrid coffee strains to withstand certain types of disease and climate change related issues.

I'm hopefully optimistic about things. We just may need to pivot as a business. I think there will still be coffee plants left, but the specialty coffees that we are used to getting take extremely unique growing environments like high altitude and volcanic soils. Just a few degrees in temperature and these coffee will no longer grow. Robusta coffees are much heartier plants and grow in less unique climates, but it's much more bitter and is typically what you'd find in coffees like Folgers.

A world with bitter coffee is still worth living in and loving.

Collapse Now, and Avoid the Rush

This book title-turned-slogan, coined by John Michael Greer, sums up both the inevitably of collapse and the reasons we ought to create a collapse-aware and ready food system. The food system paradigm shift we have been advocating thus far is collapse-compatible. Indeed, it is the kind of thing that makes the most sense because we know collapse is already happening. We could finish the book and advise you on how to make decisions, spend money, and do your best in the system as it is, and for a short time – perhaps even the remainder of some adult human lives – that would seem helpful. But, if we care about the generations left to reap what agricapitalism has sown, we can't stop there. Young people, people in those regions that have benefited the least from economic development and stand to bear the worst impacts of the climate crisis (often called double-exposed regions), future people, and all the other beings who live on this Earth need us to move toward relational, collaborative, empathic, and sustaining food systems.

The ideas around collapse have been nibbling at the corners of our consciousness and our research for years. In fields as diverse as ecological economics, supply chain logistics, geography, energy, political science, psychology, and even in science fiction writing, collapse has been the elephant in the room dancing on the table in a bright purple tutu that we really should not have been able to avoid for so long. When Nicole and her team at Sterling College were putting together EcoGather, a community co-created digital learning network, collapse was in the air. (We will get into EcoGather in Chapter Five and how it is all at once an example of targeted universalism, cosmolocalism, and uses connected ways of knowing to share agrelational moves across time and space.)

However, when designing EcoGather, they knew from studying David Fleming that "Large-scale problems do not require large-scale solutions; they require small-scale solutions within a large-scale framework." [134] Indeed, the project started out by building courses with Shaun Chamberlin using David Fleming's work. Shaun's concept of Dark Optimism – a combination of being "unashamedly positive about what kind of a world humanity could create, and unashamedly realistic about how far we are from creating it today" – is important to keep in mind. For Shaun and his students, Dark Optimism diffuses the fear that can prevent us from seeking hard truths: "By exploring the unknown we can see it for what it is, rather than what we might fear it to be. Where there is darkness present we face it with an indomitable belief in the potential of humankind." [135] This helps us to confront hard truths with a sense of possibility, which dulls the feelings of helplessness that collapse might otherwise engender.

As the EcoGather team got more comfortable talking about collapse, first amongst themselves and then in wider circles with collaborators, they became convinced that confronting collapse was essential to food systems education and change. Thus, they set about highlighting the signs of collapse where they were already apparent, convening people eager to be together in the "space between stories," as in Shaun's work, and exchanging the kinds of time-honored knowledge and skills that ecological and civilizational decline make relevant once again.

Along the way, they began listening to a podcast named Breaking Down: Collapse. [136] This podcast is just two midwestern guys who are, happily and helpfully, unlikely candidates for anything highly academic, theoretical, or out there. These guys normalize the idea of collapse and break it down into digestible chunks. Listening while driving through rural Vermont, Nicole was sucked in by the normalcy of the whole thing. Hearing the hosts, Kory and Kellan, go to and stay with the trouble reminded her that the rest of us better not shy away from it. Michelle listened to the podcast with an 80-year-old friend as they drove across the country and, to her surprise, her friend, a physicist and realist, did not question any of the conclusions Kory and Kellan came to. In fact, he helpfully added in commentary from his long and very interesting life to support their points.

Over the past two decades, there has been much ado about food system adaptation and sustainability – including in response to the climate crisis. But precious little of the theorizing or doing takes collapse seriously or addresses it head on. While we might have done better to reckon with collapse at the start of "the food movement," late is better than too late – and never is not an option.

To fully understand the intersecting set of highly complex systems and driving forces that set us up for and accelerate collapse could take several lifetimes. But even with the bird's eye view that follows, you will see elements and flows familiar from our tour of the food system.

In complexity, everything depends on everything. It is not possible to catalog all the ways we are connected. Channels as old as the water cycle and as new as the internet link up the whole world. Some part of almost everything in the room you're sitting in came from somewhere else, often through complex supply chains. The thread of complexity created just by you reading this would travel around the world several times before you even got to us sitting here writing. Complexity is mind-boggling, but it is not necessarily bad. Complexity is a feature of natural and living systems. Here's the rub: The things we did as we complexified human systems degraded natural and living systems to the point where they now lack the complexity to maintain dynamic balance. Extracting from the Earth and its ecosystems diminishes resilient capacity and also changes the way planetary systems play with each other. For a pretty common example, a carbon dioxide-filled atmosphere warms the oceans, which in turn creates massive hurricanes and typhoons that, among other devastating impacts, draws salt water onto land and renders soils infertile.

Industrial societies, economies, and agriculture were all brought to us by coal, petroleum, and natural gas – three types of sunlight storage that take millions of years to form and must be extracted from the Earth. We probably don't need to tell you that these fossilized energy sources are in short and finite supply. As they run out – and more urgently, as we must drastically reduce our reliance on them to avoid accelerating the climate crisis – exponential economic growth cannot be sustained. And capitalism isn't a system that can idle. Like an airplane that must keep moving to stay aloft, capitalist economies require growth or else they plummet.

Those trying to keep the plane in the air are banking on a transition to deceptively named "renewable energy" technologies – yet another set of good ideas that will buy some time but won't save us because of the still-extractive and short-termist thinking driving much of its current implementation. Renewables have been positioned as the silver bullet that will slay climate change,[137] but the generation and storage technologies developed to date are reliant upon minerals and rare elements, which must be mined (extracted) and are in even shorter supply than fossil fuels.[138] Once wrestled out of the ground, itself an energy-intensive and destructive process, toxic metals like mercury, barium, lead, chromium and cadmium threaten human and ecosystem health. Renewable energy sources can help decrease greenhouse gas emissions and air pollution – this will keep a growth-oriented global economy in the air for longer than the dwindling and climate-poisoning supply of fossil fuels will. But allowing an extractive economy to chug along won't renew the soils, forests, oceans that power the planet's life-supporting capacity.[139] As degrowth advocate Jason Hickel succinctly summed it, "A growth-obsessed economy powered by clean energy will still tip us into ecological disaster."

According to our economics and energy expert, it's all well and good to fix energy production, but if you don't also look at transportation and industrial processes, you are also missing the point. However, he points out that with the right goals, a lot of things that are "not good enough" on their own woven together to serve a relational goal can help. But the goals matter.

The food system can, in some ways, be thought of as a secondary energy system. Its outputs are how we supply humans with energy and are even measured in calories, units of energy measurement. All agriculture is premised on harnessing and converting the energy of the sun into forms usable by living organisms. Plants are the real heroes because they photosynthesize – turning sunlight into substances that animals, including humans, can eat. Industrial agriculture uses, among other inputs, massive amounts of non-renewable energy to produce the kind of energy our bodies can use. Moreover, modern diets in wealthy and rapidly developing economies consist of foods that are not energy efficient to produce. Consider, for example, a sirloin steak. To produce every one calorie of beef in the steak you throw on your barbeque, a cow consumes 25 calories of feed (usually a combination of grasses humans can't eat and grains that we can).[140] A 25:1 ratio is hardly efficient, and that's before we even account for the additional energy used in processing, packaging, chilling, transporting and grilling that steak. Energy scarcity will have cascading impacts, one of which could easily be food scarcity.

Extraction and cheap energy enabled economic growth. As economies grew, they also complexified. Many humans put their magnificent minds to the task of making profits from profits, which resulted in a financial system that is incomprehensible to most of us. Complexity in the financial system is not strictly necessary unless the goal is to make more money for the people and nations that already have heaps of it. The financial crisis of 2008 and the crazy combination of inflation, record earnings for corporations, and buy-backs for shareholders in 2022 are ready examples of how out of our control that system has become. Those of us who haven't learned the secret handshakes of futures speculators and derivatives traders understand these phenomena to be signs of an economy that has nothing to do with getting ahead through hard work. The knowledge of how rigged this kind of economy is contributes to more fierce polarization, exploitation by politicians (especially the neo-facsist variety), and political turmoil that spreads across the globe like a virus. This sets off a self-reinforcing cycle of breaking, hardening, and retreat, which gets locked in through algorithmically constructed news feeds and entertainment that keeps our attention by amping up outrage. The end result is isolation and despair – conditions which are anathema to relationship but also can be remedied by it.

These factors, and more you can research if you are interested, lead to catabolic collapse, which John Michael Greer explains as the way that human societies on the way down cannibalize their own infrastructure, maintaining themselves for the present by denying themselves a future. (Fun fact: catabolism is the type of metabolic activity in an organism that enables the breakdown of complex molecules to release energy. In other words, it's the biochemical process that follows eating and digestion. We told you everything connects to food.) In a catabolic scenario, all of the surplus capital that the dying system(s) created for a small number of people rapidly becomes less useful. In one of her many mic-drop moments, Naomi Klein said: "What the climate needs to avoid collapse is a contraction in humanity's use of resources; what our economic model demands to avoid collapse is unfettered expansion. Only one of these sets of rules can be changed, and it's not the laws of nature."[141]

Be Collapse Aware

Let's take a breath to normalize and stabilize this situation. It can be fear-inducing for all of us and trauma-inducing for many. All of the possible emotional responses are normal and we have had or seen them all. However, being collapse-aware gives us back the correct amount of control humans should have. We can legitimately control our own responses, our choices, what we decide to do next, and how we relate to each other. If we do, we won't be crushed by collapse. We'll be able to move along the curves of decline.

If we don't confront and prepare, mentally and relationally, for collapse, we'll find ourselves careening and crashing over a period of one to three centuries. We'd rather not do that. We'd rather move along the curves of decline, experiencing the crises and understanding that they are part of a process. It's always worse when each individual event feels confusing and unrelated. It is exhausting to ask over and over again, "Why is this happening?" Those creeping feelings of unease that come when you hear about supply chain issues on the radio, when you can't seem to find pasta in any of your grocery stores, or when we could not find dinner in Burlington are how we perceive the low rumblings of a destabilizing system. This is what some systems thinkers call weak signals.

We can start listening and responding to the weak signals – and the collapse theorists – without constantly catastrophizing and fixating on worst-case scenarios. It can actually help to recognize that no one knows for certain what the future will bring – when, where, or how. Collapse may happen in noisy fits and starts or it may be slow and plodding. We may find ways to sensibly simplify some systems before they slip out of our control and we may not be able to salvage others. Either way, if we begin voluntarily simplifying our systems and our lives, we'll be better able to keep our footing through the slips and slides of collapse. Choosing to let go of things we don't need and to build alternative economies that don't rely on growth may feel restrictive at first, but it is categorically different from the economic dynamics of a recession, which is what happens when an existing economy that requires growth to stay in the air contracts and free fall follows.

Collapse is not a conspiracy theory. We're not claiming that a nefarious individual actor or faction is pulling puppet strings or playing dominoes. There is no globally coordinated strategy to make humanity crash out. No one is doing this to us except for maybe the humans in history who made a few centuries of selfish choices – and we can't castigate them too harshly for lacking foresight or being products of their time. We don't waste our time on finger-pointing because we're not going to affix blame, hold a recall vote, or oust a government to forestall collapse. We are all complicit in various ways.

Complicity doesn't feel good, but it is also not the worst news. It means that when faced with collapse we have choices and some agency. We, the collapse-aware, can find and stay with each other in the trouble. We can gently share what we've learned to help others get a better sense of what's happening and use instability to re-form our communities. (We know this is possible because many of us only got to know our neighbors during COVID-19 lockdowns.) We do not have to consign ourselves to futures of chaos, misery, and privation – we can find meaning, comfort, and even pleasure in choosing to de-complexify certain parts of our lives and investing in the experiences and relationships that will enable us to cope. John Michael Greer says that "Starting right away to practice the skills, assemble the resources, and follow the lifeways that will be the key to survival in a deindustrializing world offers the best hope of getting through the difficult years ahead with some degree of dignity and grace." We can do that when we follow the principles of relationality in the next chapter. Consider how you want to live and what you can simplify. Begin now.

Surrogate Scenario Building through Sci Fi

COVID-19 opened the doors to the future and set us on a new path. The writer Arundhati Roy wrote from India on April 3, 2020, that the pandemic was a portal: "Whatever it is, coronavirus has made the mighty kneel and brought the world to a halt like nothing else could. Our minds are still racing back and forth, longing for a return to 'normality', trying to stitch our future to our past and refusing to acknowledge the rupture. But the rupture exists. And in the midst of this terrible despair, it offers us a chance to rethink the doomsday machine we have built for ourselves. Nothing could be worse than a return to normality."[142]

The slide into the future is here. We are not going back to whatever we had come to feel was normal, despite efforts to do just that. We need to figure out how to live. In the next chapter, we outline principles that can reset the interconnections in food systems so that they become more relational and shift the purpose back to what it was at the dawn of agriculture – sharing sustenance. A framework for relationality helps us to create cultures of survival. The question remains in all of our minds: how will it feel to be there?

When we talked about storytelling as surrogate scenario building on a personal level, we meant that stories help you make individual decisions without having to live through the consequences of many rounds of bad decisions. Science fiction, especially dystopian and utopian climate fiction, spins surrogate scenarios on a systems level. It lets us see the systems changes in action and understand their repercussions. Sci-Fi also subtly trains us to scenario-plan. It helps us to identify the skills that we (along with our kin and descendants) may need to live and even thrive during near-future periods of contraction, challenge, or decline.

You may not be a science fiction fan, but don't skip over this section. What science fiction does for us, that we all desperately need, is play out alternative futures that give us possibilities and systems knowledge that are not being offered to us right now by any other means. Science fiction is a way to model the future and change certain factors and understand the impacts on us and our world. So, while you are thinking *Star Trek*, we are thinking huge systems modeling through literature with a heaping side of scenario planning. Even legal scholars are using sci fi to play out potential futures; Bennett Capers, for example, explores policing and technology through Afrofuturism. Explaining his unconventional approach, the law professor said, "It's easy to be pessimistic about the status quo. But smart people should start planning now for a future world in order to better map a way toward it. It's important to have a vision."

Science fiction and fantasy writer N.K. Jemisin agrees that science fiction can model the future with scenarios played out for specific changes. Those changes are what she calls the "X Factor."[143] Playing with an X Factor changes the world into a future scenario and helps us see different outcomes. Science fiction stories vary tremendously based on how the author's aims, preoccupations, and positionality interact with their chosen X Factor. For example, in *The Parable of the Sower*, Octavia E. Butler traverses both urban racialized capitalist dystopia and agrarian utopia, weaving the beauty of the sacred through it all. Throughout that book, she explores both the skills we will need to develop in the future and the kinds of relationships that will liberate us. The X factor is almost indistinguishable from our present – but *Parable of the Sower* was written in 1993.

By contrast, Kim Stanley Robinson's *New York 2140*, set in a partially underwater New York City, gets us thinking about the economic and technical changes that sustain life under radically changed conditions and could lead to more just societies. The X Factor is underwater New York (very plausible) and the solutions the book offers are technological and economic. In his *Ministry for the Future*, Kim Stanley Robinson takes a look at what kinds of changes would happen in our economic system if the goal we focused on was climate stabilization. In interviews, he goes deep into Keynesian economic theory, which while interesting to us climate geeks, becomes much more comprehensible when you see it played out across the world in his novel.

For her part, Margaret Atwood explores how dystopias might form in the *MaddAddam* trilogy. Atwood's X factor is the total collapse of society and she offers up an eerie vision of a biotech-driven food system that produces nutrient bars and chickienobs, an unappetizing future merger of industrial meat and genetic modification.

Nnedi Okorafor places the African diasporic experience in the center of science fiction, where it belongs. Keenly aware that science fiction often uses and abuses tropes of the global African diaspora, placing Black characters in contexts of enslavement, colonization, genocide, war, sexual violence, famine and disease, Okorafor gives us an X factor of placing the focus on these communities. She pens Afrofuturist stories that explore explorations of how energy, food, technology, and politics intersect to save her characters. One of Michelle's teachers in graduate school, the science fiction author Samuel R. Delaney said it this way: "Science fiction isn't just thinking about the world out there. It's also thinking about how that world might be—a particularly important exercise for those who are oppressed, because if they're going to change the world we live in, they—and all of us—have to be able to think about a world that works differently."[144]

These are just a few examples of how science fiction can be a modeling and scenario planning exercise. Imogen Malpas writes in the *Lancet* "[T]he unexpected strength of climate fiction lies in its capacity to communicate compelling narratives, not just about the risk of climate collapse, but also about opportunities to rethink our economic and social infrastructure in order to avert disaster at the root. Moreover, where climate science remains dominated by socially privileged voices, climate fiction presents a vast swathe of perspectives that are particularly valuable when analysing how environmentally-oriented policy design impacts the non-Western, lower-income populations of colour that show up less frequently in the headlines."[145] We can learn a lot when we immerse ourselves in the speculations of those with lived experiences that are different from those who have most heavily influenced the world systems we live in now.

Your "Topia"

Nicole's eldest son asked us one night "Is our future going to be a dystopia?" We each had different answers, but they fit together like puzzle pieces. Nicole said, "That's up to us and the choices we make to help other people, to prepare, to learn new things, to share what we know and to create community." Michelle answered "Your 'Topia' is up to you. As things change in big ways, you may get to be outside more, fish, swim in lakes, grow food, hike with the dogs. You do fewer standardized tests and more making. For you, that's a utopia. Other people will probably lose things that are important to them, maybe even things they can't survive without. For them, it will be a dystopia." He looked at us seriously and said, "Okay, but will this happen in my lifetime?" We both replied, "It's happening right now." He found that reassuring in a way that adults might not, but we got it. Right now feels weird but manageable, so maybe we can do this.

Living inside late-stage complex systems involves a whole lot of the things that suck up our time and energy, attention and resources. As these distracting obligations and narcotic distractions die back, we will find more spaces and places to sow the seeds of relationality. And what we need will grow in that space, so long as we tend to it. After converting the energy of our spirits and the sun, there will be plenty enough pleasure, meaning, and joy.

Chapter 4

Dispatches from a Relational Future

Response to collapse necessitates relationality and, specifically, agrelational food systems. We need a more holistic approach to agriculture that seeks to align farming with both natural processes and the needs of local communities, as well as to provide decent livelihoods, preserve or restore healthy habitats, and encourage resilience. We are not basing this desire for relationality on personal preference, optimism, or any other dewy-eyed or bleeding-heart tendencies we may have. The hard cold facts of collapse and the need for system change are what brought us to this understanding.

We've reached the point in the book where start addressing the "how." This chapter offers principles that can ground and guide us as we set about shaping change in the food system. If you are a policy maker or an activist in the world of political change, take these principles and apply them to the policies you are advocating to enact. If you are in business, consider how these principles impact the way you choose to work. If you are a student, this may be a guide to how to focus your studies, and if you are working in an NGO or nonprofit, your organization can take a look at the work you do and use these principles to assess your next steps. The point is to shape the interventions we make to bring about the world we need.

Where do you intervene in a system to make the most difference? We go back to our favorite systems thinker, Donella Meadows. She famously identified the mindsets or what we might call paradigms as especially impactful ways to shape change. These paradigms function at a high level – they are not the details of how things get done but the goals of the system, or what we would call the culture of the system. We believe that the culture of a system is the originating force behind the rules, the connections, and then even the details on how it gets played out. This is because "paradigms are the sources of systems. From them, from shared social agreements about the nature of reality, come system goals and information flows, feedbacks, stocks, flows and everything else about systems." You can do other things like share information about the system, change the rules for subsidies or regulations, try to change who is in power – and you may see some desired improvements as a result. None of those changes will make as much difference as aiming at the paradigm.[146] No other intervention is harder, but culture or paradigm shift is what makes change happen so don't believe anyone who tells you it can be as easy as just changing your buying preferences.

Drawing inspiration from philosopher of science Thomas Kuhn who coined the term "paradigm shift," Donella Meadows also told us how to approach this awesome task.

First and consistently, you **point out the anomalies and failures of the old paradigm**. We did that in Chapter Two, mobilizing statistics that back up what you already know from your own experience – the food system is not working well for enough people, for the land, and for other living beings. We need to admit to ourselves and each other that the system, which is a combination of broken and brutalizing, has already become unmanageable for some people. At the rate we are going, it will be unmanageable for all of us way too soon.

Second, you **operate audaciously from the new paradigm**. We support grounded hope. We would not be writing this book if we did not genuinely believe that change is possible when we improve the quality of relationships throughout the food system. So, we start doing it now, and out loud, and with joy and song. We want people to hear what we are doing and feel inspired to sing along, adding their own parts and harmonies.

Third, you **support people who embrace the new paradigm** to rise into places of public visibility and power. There is a power structure. Though we say we need to work around it, we also need to bring it up to speed. The philosopher Hannah Arendt says that we can never depend on the power structure to start the changes we need, but we can bring them along and put people in power to support us.

Fourth, you **prioritize putting your attention on those who are receptive**. When we talk about change there is a curve. There are early adopters – the first brave souls to groove to this music. (You might be among them if you are reading this book.) Then, there are early majority folks who see what the early adopters are doing, like what they see, and step onto the dance floor. Finally, a crowd of people will begin to pick up what others are laying down – to understand the change. All of those people are open to the thrumming of this new beat and start to get down with it. But not everyone is a joiner. There will be a percentage of people who, for all their own reasons, will never listen, or will actively disregard what you are saying. So, never mind the party poopers or crashers – the reactionaries and zealous opponents. Build coalitions with "active change agents and with the vast middle ground of people who are open-minded." These useful general guidelines have informed this book and our work in the food system – and we've needed to pair them with more details about how to specifically make shifts toward relationality.

All of the qualities, ethics, or processes and principles we are about to list as the characterizing features of a relational food system need not be in place all at once. Resist the urge to treat what follows as a checklist or certification scheme – there's no need to or real value in ticking boxes to prove that you are credibly "performing" relational food systems. You don't need the gold star, you need information, connection, stories, and the agency to make the right choices for your context and community. This is your "Topia" and you get to choose what to make it.

A Few Caveats

We are not against exchanging goods for money. Agrelational approaches do not prohibit the buying and selling of food. Though such exchanges may look and feel different in the future. We are not all going to raise our own cows, make our own cheese, slaughter and butcher our own meat, and make our own shoes. We will need to organize those activities differently to meet different criteria for success and with access to different resources than we have now. For example, currently four giant conglomerates control the entire meat industry. Ranchers are getting ground up themselves by these behemoths.[147] A better alternative would be to keep the money, value, and labor locally and let people get fairly compensated for that work by their community. Doing this in a robust way breaks the stranglehold of agricapitalism while also letting us buy meat from people we now have an opportunity to actually know.

This might sound like a dressed-up version of "buy local," which is appealing but as enacted in the United States, has so far failed to be transformational. This is because we've been trying to rebuild local and regional food systems within the old agricapitalist paradigm, which is set up to reward large scale, optimizing, and efficiency-obsessed models. We've largely left the success of local "up to the market" – throwing those farmers and food providers with relational impulses into the Colosseum of agricapitalism and expecting them to fend for themselves, all while shooting steroidal subsidies into the already muscular arms of "conventional ag." Who would you bet on?

For local and regional food to have a fair chance, four conditions must exist. We need to:

(1) Advance policies with relational goals;

(2) structure public programs and spending in ways that encourage and reward relationships (that bridge, not break);

(3) pull back on subsidies and arrangements that prop up the unsustainable and harm-causing "conventional" model; and

(4) resource relational alternatives so that they can stand a chance in a sector where competition is still king.

We can't expect local and regional players to show up collaboratively when the name of the game is no-holds-barred competition and the hulking incumbents are being juiced up. Because we're starting with such an uneven playing field, we must first level things out. Pricing in externalities, incentivizing collaboration.

We know how impossible policy change feels to the average person. We felt that way when we set out to create a farmworkers rights bill and then support the legislators who introduced it in Colorado. And, what we took away from the experience was that it is ugly, you don't necessarily want to see how the sausage gets made, but it was not impossible. When we look at Belo Horizonte and the policy changes made in Brazil in Chapter Five, you will see how their changes supported small farms, increased nutrition, ended hunger, created community, and incentivized businesses. So, this is not only possible but has already happened and is now part of our history.

This is not theoretical but very practical. Our coffee guy, Josh, brought us back to how the relational choices we make add up. After we wrote the last chapter, he cheered us with some ground-truth, offering his vision of what a relational future for the coffee trade may be like when the climate crisis kicks into higher gear:

My two cents is that by just being born on this planet, each one of us is going to leave some sort of negative impact on the world. But it's up to us to decide how much. The Coffee Ride isn't a perfect business, but I can sleep at night knowing that we are putting in a solid effort to do the right thing and provide something that makes the community feel good being a part of. Small things can add up.

Think of what follows as a collection of signals and principles we receive from the future that will resonate over time to help us survive. We can't tell the future but we can certainly see what is emerging. We can and audaciously point out the successes. As we move through the rest of the book, we will share stories of already existing communities, projects, thinkers, moments – all of which are stronger signals. We will look back on them from a more fully relational future and say: "That is the story of how we got here."

Cosmolocal Approaches

What exactly is Cosmolocalism? Our colleague Heidi Myers insists that it sounds like a tasty cocktail, but past that, she was baffled by our pretty academic attempts at describing it. Her questions and then our responses were much better than any other way we have ever tried to explain this. And it makes sense. Instead of two wonky geeky food people talking inside a bubble, the interaction was relational and Heidi, who is not a food systems person, was the perfect person because she was not 100 percent bought into the idea – though the cocktail kept her interested.

Heidi: You keep using this word, but I'm still struggling to understand cosmolocalism.

Nicole: Under global neoliberal and extractive capitalism, the motives are profit and economic growth, right? So you take things from wherever they are and can be extracted or can be produced most cheaply and sell them wherever they can yield the greatest profits. So that means that countries rich in resources and people end up impoverished from extraction. Then there are systems of enclosure and exclusion, like privatization through intellectual property, which mean that when humans figure something out, that knowledge gets privatized and serves the interests of existing capital. So, this is how we get to a global economy that takes things from "poor" countries (which are actually quite rich in resources or labor) and then holds tightly to the capacity to make things that get sold all around the world.

Heidi: Not good. And I totally get why you'd want to stop that kind of trade, but what is the difference between cosmolocal and local?

Nicole: So, localism basically says: Forget Globalization. We will do as much as possible locally and we won't worry about the people or places in other parts of the world. This has appeal and feels safer. But, it is also limiting and parochial, meaning that we can't learn from each other or benefit by trading the things that are truly unique. And it is pretty counter to sharing knowledge or care for each other. Plus it reinforces the disparities that exist already. If you don't create it from scratch, you don't have access to it. So it could mean reinventing the wheel all around the world because we didn't share the idea of the wheel or it could mean no coffee or other tropical products in North America because that doesn't grow here.

Heidi: You want the best of both, or the least damaging from both? And with fair compensation not exploitation?

Nicole: Cosmolocalism is different. It basically says: we are all connected across the globe, both through our common humanity and also because we've figured out how to do things technologically that allow us to move materials, information, biological matter (like viruses), and physical matter (like CO_2) everywhere. We can't deny the connections. Instead, we should share what can be shared (like knowledge) openly, and trade materials much more judiciously. We are actually stronger when we learn from and care about each other. But our exchanges need to be more relational, less transactional.

Heidi: So cosmolocalism is like maple syrup versus sugar? Maple syrup is shared or for sale but maintains value, skill, land-based livelihoods in our region, etc. Sugar on the other hand is cheap, exploitative, majorly mass-produced, and mimicked?

Nicole: You are starting to get it. Cosmolocalism says local is primal, sensory, and as real as it gets. So for Vermonters, maple syrup. We inhabit particular places on the Earth – and only one at a time. We are part of our place(s), like it or not. Our locales shape lived experience and personal memory. We are there. Present, but influenced by the past and responsible for the future. At the same time, universality transcends our lived experience and whispers to us of our common being as humans. This is the basis of mutual recognition, mutual care. It moves us beyond our limited, local and personal spheres and substantiates our sense of a common good, a common future, and a common responsibility.

Heidi: But is the syrup in "the Cosmolocal" when we make it as a cocktail? Seriously, do we hoard all the syrup?

Nicole: Stick with the syrup for a minute. There might be ways we go about caring for our sugar bushes and making syrup here in the Northeast Kingdom of Vermont that communities elsewhere could learn from to tap their own trees, maple or otherwise, so it's good to share what we know and how we do things. And if they don't have access to a reasonable alternative in their part of the world, it makes sense to trade the extra we have. But we aren't taxing our trees, which offer us so much more than just sugar and are our kin in this place, to generate tons of excess as cheaply as we can. More than likely there is something that makes other parts of the world sweet in their own ways – dates, honey, cane, beets, sorghum, birch, coconut. In those places, those sweeteners would be relied on first and most, but not exclusively.

Heidi: Well, what about things we can't touch and don't make locally?

Nicole: Okay, instead of syrup, imagine a global network of mutually supportive local communities making mindful and appropriate use of digital information and communication technologies to share and exchange the non-material resources that can and should flow freely around the globe: knowledge, ideas, practices, skills, innovations, and culture. Material resources – tangible things – are sometimes exchanged among and between them, but only to the extent that they are socially and ecologically sustainable and not primarily for the purpose of making a profit (though potentially as a way to support decent livelihoods and mutual thriving of both trading partners). This arrangement offers an alluring alternative to the kind of totalizing globalization that drowned out local cultures and subsumed place-based economies into a homogenized global system that extracts, exploits, and erodes the planet's life-supporting capacity. At the same time, intentional sliding between the local and the universal avoids parochialism, isolationism, fetishization, and selfishness that can come with localization and open it up to caricature and ridicule. Cosmolocalism invites us to be where we are, to give our places and communities the precious gift of our care and attention, while also reminding us that ours is not the only location, culture or people on the planet that matters. It honors the common causes among peoples by creating knowledge commons that transcend place.

This is where Heidi decided she really got it, and we realized we had succeeded better in explaining it in text messages than we had originally. (If you are friends with Nicole, you get used to paragraphs-long texts that use words like "substantiate" and "privatize".)

Nevertheless, it's also worth sharing a bit about where these concepts came from. In its earliest and most practical forms, this concept combines globally open-source design with local or regional production to get the best of both worlds. When ideas are open, human creativity is shareable, making stuff happens locally, and the material goods we rely on can be made, adapted and maintained within our particular contexts, the relationships between producers and consumers get reshuffled in really interesting ways.

These core ideas from the design-manufacture space have been extended into the social innovation and community development discourse, where their more lyrical name, cosmolocalism, is often used. Cosmolocalism envisions radically different kinds of linkages between local and global communities than those that have formed – and strangled peoples and places – under global and neoliberal capitalism. The remix spun by cosmolocalism encourages us to make some sweet, sliding moves between locality and universality. Its rhythm drives a deep respect for the local as our most important social and ecological sphere; its melody sings of the potential for global networking beyond the logics and narrow incentives of capitalism.[148] Its chorus proclaims its characteristics: small, local, open, and connected. We'll dance to that!

Its most enthusiastic proponents believe that cosmolocalism could lead the way for a transition to post-capitalist, commons-centric economies and societies where value is shared widely and community autonomy flourishes. Cosmolocalism's focus on building distributed systems and resilient infrastructures that enable us to reduce the distance between production and consumption seems particularly suited to creating the conditions for relational food systems without being anti-innovation.

An early and intriguing example is Farm Hack, a worldwide community of farmers (and others) that build and modify their own tools, which was originally incubated and launched by the National Young Farmers Coalition, the Greenhorns and GreenStart in 2011, and is now an independent 501c3.

In its own words: *We believe that greater knowledge sharing will lead to better tools, skills and systems to build successful, resilient farms. Open-source seeds, breeds and technology are the fastest way to accelerate innovation and adaptation, and ensure an equitable, diverse agricultural landscape. By documenting, sharing and improving farm tools, we can improve the productivity and viability of sustainable farming and local manufacturing. The result will be healthy land, abundant food, successful farm businesses and invigorated local economies.*[149]

Members of the Farm Hack community share their innovations, or "hacks," regularly online and at in-person meet ups because they believe firmly that better farmers work together. That said, the community is not limited to farmers; it is open to engineers, roboticists, designers, architects, fabricators, tinkerers, programmers, hackers motivated to help farmers solve puzzles. Hacker culture and sustainable agriculture are easy kin. Moreover, the rise of hacker culture and the revival of small-scale sustainable farming both emerged in response to capitalist enclosure and firms' outlandish exertions of control over their customers' access to basic technologies, tools, and parts. With these common motivations, it is no wonder that Farm Hack's repository of tool designs and agricultural knowledge has rapidly grown to include both open source designs for equipment and tools and documentation of farming technologies and practices. Whether you are looking to construct a simple pig shelter, make a device to separate garlic cloves, rig up a bicycle powered thresher, find open-source crop planning software, or build a multi-function automated farmbot, Farm Hack's tool library will show you the way. Its collaborative, relational culture of problem solving and supportive community allow knowledge to move among farmers who are very much tied to and invested in the wellbeing of their places.

Importantly, because Farm Hack set design principles that prioritize an eco-relational approach to agriculture, the innovations that emerge allow farmers to hack their way into more harmonious relationships with their land. As Farm Hackers teach each other "better ways of harnessing the complex biogeochemical flows of atmospheric carbon, water, and nitrogen into productive and resilient agroecosystems,... emphasis shifts from efficient extraction of resources to skilled regeneration of resources using all available knowledge. The focus becomes improving rather than diminishing the natural resource base."[150] This allows farmers to be in reciprocal relationship with each other and the land. Check them out at www.farmhack.com as there are just too many cool things on offer there to pick one.

Connected Knowing

As we confirmed when we discovered Farm Hack, knowledge and knowing is crucial to our becoming relational. The ways of knowing that will inform choices, decisions, and planning in agrelational food systems are those that place people, land, and climate above profit. Our food system is not a data point. In fact, you can't eat data, so we can be sure it's not food. Not even metaphorically like "food for the soul." The ways of knowing that will inform choices, decisions, and planning in agrelational food systems are those that put people, land, and climate above profit.

Connected Knowing comes out of feminist ethics and the study of how we learn and accrue information. As we move into an agrelational food system and tend its cosmolocal knowledge commons, an abundance of time-honored wisdom and emergent insights will be shared. It is, therefore, important to consider how we ought to encounter knowledge – how we treat the very experience of knowing.

Connected knowers are "not dispassionate, unbiased observers." They deliberately bias themselves in favor of what they are examining. They try to get inside it and form an intimate attachment to it. The heart of connected knowing is imaginative attachment: trying to get behind the other person's eyes and "look at it from that person's point of view."[151] To practice connected knowing in food systems work, we must talk to people, explore the life of plants, follow the biological processes, and say "yes" to all of it. We do not judge, we take life on life's terms. We retain our capacity for critical thinking (a form of separate knowing), but we don't jump to criticize because we are also feeling with the system. By empathizing and believing before we doubt and critique, we can develop richer understandings. This stance helps us to address the complexity of the world. It also prevents us from dismissing the bits that are inconvenient to us and reflexively rejecting insights offered by those whose interests and priorities we suspect may rub up against our own.

The thinker and activist Claire Nelson offers a values-based way to make smarter decisions that reads to us like a manifesto for integrated thinking – the kind that toggles between connected knowing and critical thinking, offering the benefits of both emotion and reason. Hers is a way to put the theory into practice when we are trying to shape change, especially in systems. In her book *Smart Futures for a Flourishing World*, Claire provides a SMART framework of questions to promote curious conversations:

1. "How is this (Policy? Program? Project?) I am designing a Sustainable System?"
2. "Are we using meaningful metrics and not the ones that created the problem?"
3. "Do we give all the parts of the system agency, a voice, do we take them into consideration as individuals as well as a whole?"
4. "Are we building resilience into the system for everyone and not just for economics?"
5. "Is the technology we are using relationally transformational or just technologically transformational? Is it going to improve the outcomes for the whole system or just for those in power?" [152]

Claire brings connected knowing and an ethos of relationality to development work in Caribbean nations and for all our futures. She's an engineer by training and worked for over 30 years at the Inter-American Development Bank. Yet, even after having been steeped in detached ways of knowing for so long, when Claire speaks to a group, she draws them in by dropping them right in the middle of a story. She uses story to both create connection and encourage suspension of judgment to generate imaginative attachment. She tells her audience that she is the first Jamaican on the moon and needs help in planning an event that will take place there. On Zoom, she has a moon background and is seated as though in front of a window. Not long ago, she gave a group of our food systems students a hearty welcome and then put them to work on her moon project, which is really a cleverly disguised way to get folks thinking about how to help small island nations meet their needs. At first, the students were flummoxed. Before long, their imaginations kicked in and the possibilities expanded. They became the committee to plan the world gathering on the moon in celebration of 100 years of living in space and they began to bring themselves and their expertise, cares, and passions to Claire's undertaking. They stepped into her world, saw things from her point of view and brought themselves there to be of service. By taking these students temporarily off-planet, Claire increased their capacity to think in ways that might allow us to stay here.

When the Zoom call was over and Claire flickered out, the dazed students started identifying surprising connections between their work and the needs of the already inhabited and very threatened island nations right here on the Earth. The exercise also made them see what they knew and how they could apply it differently. By bringing them into a story that was, at once, personally intimate and expansively outer-spacey, Claire short-circuited judgment, which allowed the students to embrace the complexity of both the imaginary and real worlds she's building.

Targeted Universalism and Ground-Truthing

We get trapped in the binaries that capitalism and supremacy encourage in our thinking and how could we not? One of the binaries is "food systems need a global solution" or "food systems need a local solution." Cosmolocalism begins to address this, but it is less suited to guiding policy craft. To angle in the direction of more relational policy making, we lean into john powell's research on Targeted Universalism. Food systems are in need of both changes in goals and new policies to help us reach those goals.

The food systems "solutions" we most often read about are characterized as either global or local, innovative or traditional, expert-driven or community-based. Political differences, policy debates, resource allocations get herded into binaries. And, when we look at the food system, if we take a universal approach or a really targeted approach the same thing happens: those most in need, most marginalized, are harmed and not helped. Both approaches tend to favor one group over another and don't give the right information to establish universal goals, nor enough freedom for communities to then solve for themselves to meet those goals.

"Within a targeted universalism framework, universal goals are established for all groups concerned. The strategies developed to achieve those goals are targeted, based upon how different groups are situated within structures, culture, and across geographies to obtain the universal goal."[153]

The fixes that targeted universalism creates may be simple technical fixes or they may be wide and deep structural reforms. What they have in common is they will transform a community to meet a goal without getting caught up in the narrow preconceived notions of how things are usually done. "By emphasizing the universal goal as a way of justifying a diversity of implementation strategies, transformative change possibilities can be envisioned, pursued, and aligned."[154]

Ground-truthing is how we get to the targeted part of targeted universalism. It is a process in which researchers find out not just how the data looks but what is going on "on the ground." So in geography, they may take drone pictures of an area but they will not complete a study without validating the experience on the ground. We hear the inflection of targeted universalism when disability liberation activists insist "nothing about us without us."[155] This stance says that the people involved know what is best for them, and that no one wants to be the object of policy no one ever bothered to talk to them about.

Ground-truthing takes on a deeper meaning when we are thinking about ecological or food systems in which people, animals, insects, plants, mycelium, soil, water, air, and sunlight are stakeholders.

Universal Reciprocity

In the 1980s, the group Americans for Indian Opportunity held a series of conversations that led the founder, Comanche activist and civil rights leader LaDonna Harris, to describe "four core values which cross generation, geography and tribe," relationship, responsibility, reciprocity and redistribution, each of which "manifests itself in a core obligation in Indigenous societies."[156] It is worth reading about the 4Rs in the words of those who first expressed them:

1. Relationship is the kinship obligation, the profound sense that we human beings are related, not only to each other, but to all things, animals, plants, rocks—in fact, to the very stuff the stars are made of. This relationship is a kinship relationship. Everyone/everything is related to us as if they were our blood relatives.
2. Responsibility is the community obligation. This obligation rests on the understanding that we have a responsibility to care for all of our relatives. Our relatives

include everything in our ecological niche, animals and plants, as well as humans, even the stones, since everything that exists is alive.

3. Reciprocity is the cyclical obligation. It underscores the fact that in nature things are circular: for example, the cycle of the seasons and the cycle of life, as well as the dynamics between any two entities in relationship with each other. Once we have encountered another, we are in relationship with them.

4. Redistribution is the sharing obligation. Its primary purpose is to balance and rebalance relationships. Comanche society, for example, was an almost totally flat society, socially, politically and economically. It had many, many ways of redistributing material and social goods. In principle one should not own anything one is not willing to give away. Possessions do not own you. [157]

More recently, Chris Newman, founder of Sylvanaqua Farms and the Skywoman community, extrapolated on the idea of reciprocity, calling it Universal Reciprocity. On his Instagram feed, he shared that "Universal reciprocity is a broader understanding of reciprocal ties to all things: Our one, two, four, and many legged relations. The living, the dead, and the unborn. Spirits dwelling in the 'inanimate' (e.g., times and places). Your concept of a creator or creation. It's knowledge of how each of these is related to you does things for you and what each is owed in return. Acting on that knowledge and remaining in reciprocal balance with all things, across space and time, is universal reciprocity."[158] This is distinguishable from mutual aid, which while benevolent, is a narrower exchange between people living in the present.

Chris Newman is a farmer and social entrepreneur who figured out that the kind of change that he wanted to make wouldn't happen from his farm alone – it requires a growing community. He created a podcast that myth-busted issues around decolonization and indigenization movements. But just talking still skewed too far toward the theoretical. He saw that ending food apartheid and establishing food sovereignty would have to involve groups of people with expertise beyond farming (think: attorneys and accountants, contractors and mechanics, designers and software engineers) actually working together, not in-fighting or obsessing over imperfection. Skywoman is a place where communities can self-organize to build sovereign food systems. In fact, for Skywoman, "community is the deliverable" because "a foundation of healthy, deep, sustained, and reciprocal relationships among people can handle challenges with soil, plants, animals, air, water, ancestors, and the unborn. Weak communities will struggle on all these fronts."[159] They convene with principles of universal reciprocity and dedicate space for the organizers of food sovereignty to share stories.

Chis Newman is also a living example of the messiness of building community – especially in the context of an overculture that feeds off controversy and rewards escalation. He experienced a pretty bruising cancelation attempt. But he didn't let that rupture define him or drive him to abandon his change aims. He stayed with a very personal kind of trouble, distinguished his approach from more breaking forms of social justice praxis, and opened relational possibilities wide by naming universal reciprocity as Skywoman's guiding principle. Staying rooted in place helps us navigate the mess and get to the other side. We do not have to be perfect to make offerings of what we have learned, as Chris is doing through Skywoman.

The ethic of universal reciprocity will take us deep into relationality if we let it and live it. That said, we must take care to avoid a precious and dangerous practice: cherry-picking bits of indigenous cultures, which is currently common among people who live and farm "regeneratively" on stolen land.[160] When settlers encounter beautiful indigenous traditions involving land, seeds, and water that embody their relationship with nature, it can be tempting to replicate or riff on those same practices, untethering them from the cultures and worldviews out of which they arose. But this kind of decontextualization and appropriation will not bring us into alignment. There are no shortcuts to right relationship. Instead, reach back for traditions in the cultures of your ancestors – way back, if you need to – or listen to your intuition. The nuance and sweetness of what you find or improvise will help you experience authentic kinships and inform your work in a unique way.

Reverence

Chris Newman also talks about the importance of ceremony and about the obligation we have to revere the gifts of our myriad connections in the world. In the same post, he says:

"For me specifically a new day is repaid with tobacco :: the gift of food from the soil (the bodies of ancestors) is repaid with careful stewardship of the land :: a healthy body is repaid with attention to physical exercise and lots of water :: the unborn who will care for my great grandchildren are paid with food sovereignty work whose benefits I will not see in my lifetime :: a fiery sunset is greeted with a song."

Drawing on his Piscataway ancestry and identity, Chris Newman sees the giving and connection as ceremony, sacred acts that when practiced with intention bring something both special and essential. That this comes from Newman, who has a brash, sometimes biting sense of humor and makes plenty of irreverent posts on social media, only makes reverence more reachable. Being reverent where it matters doesn't mean we all have to float serenely through the world in perfect alignment all the time.

But absenting reverence from our work in food systems has resulted in some of the most breaking and harmful inventions of agricapitalism: monocultures sprung from seeds genetically modified to withstand dousing in harmful synthetic pesticides. Mohawk seed keeper Rowen White received this insight as she drove through the American heartland in early spring and found herself singing seed songs. She suddenly remembered that the young green shoots covering corn fields were sprouting from GMO seeds, which she and other food sovereignty seekers oppose. In that moment, she understood that it is wrong to "villainize the seeds" because "those seeds have been so exploited themselves by the larger capitalist system." She saw those seeds as a reflection of the American people and the dominant culture: "a mix of tattered origins that have been cut and spliced together... these are brokenhearted seeds being planted by brokenhearted people who have no idea of who they are and where they come from; so they make seeds that look like themselves." Rowen White strives for a food system that has inherent, whole seeds at the center and believes that making that a reality could reseed the people. "We need to reseed not only the physical seeds, the good seeds that create the foundation of our food system, but also those songs and those stories and that sense of reverence, that sense of love and connection to the food that ends up on our plates." [161]

Reverence is also alive and well outside of indigenous communities. Another moving example of putting the sacred back into the system is the work of Elizabeth DeRuff and Honoré Farm. Elizabeth, an Episcopal priest, considers herself an agricultural chaplain. Michelle interviewed Elizabeth for a faith-based change series that featured many food systems change shapers.[162] Elizabeth DeRuff created a nonprofit national network called the Growers Guild based in Marin County, California, which she sees as "farming our spiritual values" by "reknitting communities and bringing the church back into a relationship with farmers, millers, and bakers."[163] Elizabeth felt called to a piece of land near her gym, and at first, she tried to turn it into an educational farm. That failed. Upon reflection, she realized that she needed to meet people where they are. In her community, that was church kitchens. Bread breaking as a sacrament was very meaningful for Elizabeth, and she saw a need for more connections over meals to strengthen both human-to-human and spiritual connections. She ended up sowing wheat in that same field, sourcing a mill, eventually forming a loose network of local farms that now supplies her non-profit, Honoré Farm, with ancient grains for religious institutions to use in ceremony.

Honoré keeps track of how much carbon these ancient grains are sequestering, how many institutions use it, and how many farms they serve in their CSA program. But for Elizabeth, the sharing of bread in ceremony cannot be quantified. "I'm just going to speak about the Christian tradition," she said, "that we have this idea of a sacrament, which is an outward and visible sign of an inward and spiritual truth. So really, what that means to me is that the material world and the spiritual world are, are one." She pointed to Robert Capon who said, "There is a habit that plagues many so-called spiritual minds: they imagine that matter and spirit are somehow at odds with each other and that the right course for human life is to escape from the world of matter into some finer and purer (and undoubtedly duller) realm... In fact, it was God who invented dirt, onions, and turnip greens... God who, at the end of each day of creation, pronounced a resounding 'Good!' at the end of his concoctions. And it is God's unrelenting love of all the stuff of this world that keeps it in being at every moment. So, if we are fascinated, even intoxicated, by matter, it is no surprise: we are made in the image of the Ultimate Materialist."[164] For Elizabeth, bringing deep intention to the growing, milling, and baking of sacramental bread is a powerful and necessary way to honor the sacredness of all God's creation.

There is no doubt that land, relationship, food, and connection are part of the sacredness of life. Without acknowledging the sacred in any change we create we run the risk of losing what animates our world. We are not talking only about religious approaches to farming and eating, though we find halal butchers, Buddhist farmers, and Sikh theologies of food fascinating. (Exploring them would add another chapter to the book.) As we move into the agrelational paragdigm, the particularities matter less than the commonalities: approaching food in any way that also feeds our spirit makes it easier to move to and be in right relationship. Reverence is available even to those who don't participate in an organized religion. Nicole's family doesn't practice a particular religion, though they do draw upon insights from a variety of faith traditions. A very worn copy of Thich Nhat Hanh's *How To Eat* sits on the table in their kitchen. When her younger son, then a precocious three-year old, revealed that he could read by deciphering its print before a Sunday supper, he started a ritual of reverence for their family.

Pleasure

Resisting neoliberal capitalism can feel futile. One of the best – and most satisfying – ways to do so is by pursuing pleasure. The poet and activist Audre Lorde wrote "Caring for myself is not self-indulgence, it is self-preservation, and that is an act of political warfare." We need all the tools possible to fight the nihilism and disconnection that the systems in which we live use to keep us from collaborating, empathizing, caring, and building relationships.

Critical design theorist Oliver Vodeb included an entire chapter on pleasure as a practice in his very academic book on food democracy.[165] He included recipes – which are not often found in scholarly essays – because he wanted to help readers get out of their brains and into their bodies. If you want to get fancy, you can call this a somatic practice. Or you can just recognize that food and stories create delectable flows of activity and feelings between our minds and bodies. Eating popcorn watching a movie – that's the kind of pleasure bomb that happens when we experience food and story. The impact can be even stronger when the food and the stories are paired and when they connect us to our ancestors, our places, or our memories.

The ability to experience pleasure through the food system is also not a novel idea. Nor is pleasure as resistance. But we're focusing on pleasure for several reasons. First, capitalism certainly does not rely on pleasure as a way to keep score, even when it comes to food. The tomato that creates the biggest profit margin may not be the best tasting, most striking, or the juiciest. A select few restaurants around the world, the kind that make it on the 50 Best list,[166] are exquisitely attuned to pleasure, but they aren't maximally profitable, and they aren't offering pleasure to average folks. If anything, their elite status and high prices serve to make pleasure seem like it is only for the winners of the rigged economic game, a reward for serving the system.

Second, it is important to disrupt the notion that pleasure belongs locked in a binary with responsibility or social responsibility. The nature of their relationship is too nuanced to be labeled opposites. According to financial journalist Eric J. Weiner, pleasure is a way to reclaim a modicum of power within an established geography of inequitable power relationships. Living well, whatever that looks and feels like in our own contexts, allows us to rise and fight another day. "When we focus our energies on having experiences of pleasure while working to find pleasure in all kinds of experiences, we are actively resisting the soul-sucking ideology of 'neoliberal fascism' taking hold of our bodies and minds in the United States, Europe, and South America."[167] Not the kind of line we usually hear from finance writers, but we are here for it!

Some might argue, as Eric Weiner does, that the systems of oppression in which we live are worse than uncaring, they are sadistic. Being extractive isn't quite sadism, but it is born of sweeping disregard and brutal neglect for all but the narrowest of interests. Pleasure brings us back to our bodies, to relationship, and to a sense of our shared experience on this Earth. Like reverence, it defies quantification, which makes it inherently threatening to those who'd have us understand and value our existence primarily in economic terms.

But don't be caught unaware. The agricapitalists are cognizant of how powerful pleasure is – and they've tried to harness it for their own ends. Through a process they call "food optimization," food engineers change innumerable variables in a food product to find the "bliss point." When they hit it, they can manufacture a version of a food product that will "pique the taste buds enough to be alluring but [w]on't have a distinct, overriding single flavor that tells the brain to stop eating."[168] Manipulative, right? This is why highly processed foods sometimes taste really good. But bliss point is not the same as pleasure. Pringles (which Michelle has a fondness for) will always be exactly the same through the entire container – and each one will both taste good and leave you wanting another. Pleasure, on the other hand, is complex, it changes over time, it is different for different people. Ephemeral yet deeply satisfying. You can't hold on to pleasure, even if you can seek it out, you can only enjoy it when it happens and feel a deep sense of gratitude. Pleasure is impossible to commodify.

Mackenzie Faber, an EcoGather designer, discovered the importance of delight and pleasure early on in her career. While managing a small farm in Brooklyn and fighting an agitating urge to quit, she'd spy some broccoli growing near the fence or a particularly beautiful bunch of chard and get grounded. As she yanked carrots right out of the ground for lunch, an involuntary smile would spread across her face, suddenly she'd feel capable of staying in the work. Later, when she went to grad school to study food systems (with Nicole, during the pandemic), agitation was replaced by something worse: despair and anxiety.

She ordered a copy of *The Book of Delights,* Ross Gay's collection of essays written when he turned 40 and decided he would handwrite everyday about something that delighted him. This turned out to be anything but a shallow, happy-go-lucky, let's-ignore-the-problems sort of project. In the essays, he ended up grappling with all the horrible facts of life – from the racial injustice he experiences to the knowledge that every one of us will die – via the delights of everyday life. Nevertheless, the more he wrote, the more attuned his "delight radar" became, leaving him with a backlog of delights to balance the hard truths with which they co-exist. Mackenzie started reading an essay a day. It changed the way she approached her education and work. For Mackenzie, food is a source of regular delight and deep pleasure. So she allowed herself to anticipate the fruity-creamy-spicy-nutty pleasure of hummingbird cake and to unashamedly indulge in thick slices of it – even as she researched the use of forced labor in the food system. Daily delight practice helped her realize that things could be terrible and wonderful all at the same time. Developing a delight radar is a lot harder than developing a horrible-things radar, but it is the more worthy project. When Nicole invited Mackenzie to help make learning about food systems education more relational, her first move was to weave delight journaling throughout EcoGather's Food Systems Thinking course, preserving pleasure even as we reckon with painful realities.

Pleasure, far from making change harder, can recruit more folks to the cause. Political operative and spiritual teacher Reginald Hubbard, puts it this way: "Rather than view change in an adversarial manner — what if we viewed it more as a dance. Change is an essential and pleasurable part of the sacred act of creation. And besides it's easier to recruit people to a dance than a fight."

Divesting from Perfectionism,
Restoring Respect and Humility

The culture catalyzed by late-stage neoliberal extractive capitalism exhausts us with its insistence on immediacy, efficiency, optimization, and perfection – none of which are conducive to relating. It trains our attention on deficiencies – our own and others' – and then sells us something that will make us feel momentarily better. (Again, not necessarily real pleasure – but a quick hit of something that feels good.) Contemporary cultural journalist Jia Tolentino observes, "This cultural moment, and this stage of capitalism, says gratification should be instant, that efficiency is a moral good, and everything should be as cheap and easy as possible. But nothing worthwhile comes like this: easily, instantly, cheaply. Nothing we really want will leave us exempt from discomfort or difficulty. Lasting transformation requires a process that is slow and full of conflict, that implicates and imbricates us." [169] To this we would add that nothing we hope to have – and no one we can hope to shape the future with – will be perfect or live up to exacting ideals all the time.

Nothing is all good or all bad, all right or all wrong. Nicole's father has been trying to convince her of this for the better part of four decades. The lesson took a while to stick. And the good that we're trying to make isn't going to manifest immediately. Some very powerful forces in the dominant culture push us to binary thinking and assessment. We are conditioned to think in either/or, yes/no, right/wrong, or good/bad terms. Tema Okun and Kenneth Jones identified this particular form of reductionist thinking as a strong norm of white middle-class and owning-class culture and noticed that it is often accompanied by the push to perfectly perform that which has been deemed to exist on the positive or acceptable side of the binary. [170]

Those who feel most compellingly called into the change spaces tend to rush in with more passion than preparation.

They don't realize that, in doing so, they wind up tracking the dirty insistences of capitalism – easy, instant, cheap, and perfect – into relational refuges. This is especially common when activists who have internalized a rigid and rule-based social justice culture show up. They are propelled into change spaces by a combination of moral outrage and righteous indignation – which are important and mobilizing emotions in the right doses but should not be the only chords our hearts can pound out.

Contemporary social justice culture – especially as it has been influenced by outrage-oriented online discourse – can steer us into some dangerous territory. Famously canceled writer Clementine Morrigan observes that it often encourages us to "see the actions of others in the worst possible light, to take things extremely personally, to be offended easily, and to feel victimized in everyday interactions." This kind of conditioning leads to behavior that is breaking, not bridging. She clarified a whole lot when she pointed out that social justice culture – the culture and its preoccupations, not its genuine aims and intentions – is not threatening to capitalism but easily incorporated into it. Policing the language of regular folks, always asking one working-class person to Venmo another, focusing on visibility, and excoriating those who make missteps are all transactional tactics. They examine and exaggerate only what one has done lately and demand immediate and specific redress on the critic's terms. All of this sucks up energy, widens divisions, and prevents us from knitting ourselves into powerful and coalitional movements. All too often, straight-up bad behavior (by which we mean, unkind, disrespectful, and even extractive conduct) gets excused in the name of fighting an -ism. Or it is justified because the perceived transgression triggered a trauma response. While those things may be true, they don't help us stay in relationship.

Divesting from perfectionism means that we need to see escalatory breaking behavior for what it is – a thick and sticky muck of justified outrage, adjacent individual and/or collective trauma, and contemporary conditioning that keeps us stuck. It's all too easy to smear this mess everywhere and it's really hard to clean it up. Rather than stay mad at those who tracked it into our relational refuges, we must first try to help them see the mess they are making. We can also help them understand that the frequent pattern of mess-making and tidying up (also known as rupture and repair) is itself demoralizing. It burns up relational capacity and takes energy and attention away from the essential work of making alternatives real. Finally, we can explain (again) the expectations for how we handle conflict, restore, and center respect in our relational refuges. And the community as a whole must work together to uphold those values.

This patient process can only happen with those who are both willing to grow and willing to stick around. Often, though, folks stomp off as quickly as they stomped in – a sure sign that they are not prepared to stay with the trouble. But staying and having grace in the presence of imperfection are essential for getting to true social justice through interpersonal (and even interspecies) liberation.

Learning from and Living as Part of Nature

We live in an unofficial geologic era, the Anthropocene, shaped by the extractive actions of humans manipulated by capitalism. Scientists still are examining whether and to what extent evidence of our meddling is now embedded in the Earth's rock strata. But the fact that geologists are even looking makes the point: the human species is a force of nature. The question is, are we necessarily a destructive force? Homewreckers?

That can't be our character – or at least not the entirety of our arc. If you need evidence for this, you can look at some of the beautiful humans we've introduced in this book. Or better yet, at the beautiful humans in your life, the ways they give care, the ways they love. And notice how many people are trying, each in their own ways to make something better about the world.

If we can tap into that care, offer it to a wider array of lives and eco-interests, and allow it to be guided by the wisdom found in nature, it will be possible to shift into what transdisciplinary philosopher Glenn Albrecht, in his book *Earth Emotions*, calls the Symbiocene, a hoped-for next epoch in which humans cherish their place within a wider multi-species community of life, value biological and cultural diversity, and prioritize meeting their needs in ways that are mutually beneficial and supportive. To greet the dawn of this new era, we recommend a hearty breakfast of humble pie, some basic ecology lessons, and lots of time outdoors to develop a relationship with nature. You can, of course, have transformative experiences on backcountry expeditions that take you through the wildest and most pristine places remaining on the planet, though this is neither necessary nor an approachable way to get started. Begin in your backyard or in a little pocket park. Even in a landscape designed by humans, if you are attentive, you'll still be able to observe how relationships form and flux in nature.

Naturalist Melanie Choukas-Bradley, in her book *Resilience: Connecting with Nature in a Time of Crisis*, encourages people to find a "wild home," which can be right in your neighborhood, so long as it is outdoors. In fact, it shouldn't be hard to get to "[b]ecause nature connection is all about intimacy. True intimacy springs from familiarity. Traveling to faraway places is enlightening, both for enjoyment and personal growth. But it is what we tune into day to day in our familiar realms that is the most essential aspect of our experience and consciousness. Our wild homes teach us how to honor the familiar and delight in the new."[171]

If you can find a forest to visit, even a damaged one, and walk attentively through it, anthropologist Anna Lowenhaupt Tsing promises that you will be "caught by the abundance of

life: ancient and new; underfoot and reaching into the light."
She tells us to approach the forest as a story: "We might begin
by looking for drama and adventure beyond the activities of
humans. Yet we are not used to reading stories without human
heroes... We forget that collaborative survival requires cross-
species coordinations. To enlarge what is possible we need
other kinds of stories, including adventures of landscapes."[172]
Like reading science fiction, searching out the stories in the
spaces that humans do not dominate can be both expansive
and instructive. We must observe the forms, processes, and
relationships found in nature before we can emulate them.

Paying attention to relationships that don't involve humans
can also reveal some blunders and misses in how some humans
approach relationships with other humans. Our personal
relationships, of course, are nuanced and defy generalization.
But the models for human-to-human relationships that the logics
of capitalism work from are fairly flat. Indeed, economist Kate
Raworth says that "[o]ne of the most dangerous stories at the
heart of 20th century economics is the depiction of humanity as
rational economic man," a conceptual caricature who appears
all over classic economic texts and theories. Raworth sketches
a version of this economic man "standing alone, with money in
his hand, ego in his heart, a calculator in his head and nature at
his feet"; this guy "hates work, he loves luxury and he knows
the price of everything."[173] Coolly calculating, exclusively
self-interested, and competitive – this is what the capitalist
economic system tells us we need to be if we want to get ahead.
For economic man, relationships are expendable, inhibiting,
even limiting to individual liberty. This guy – and the dominant
cultural instruction to be like him – is probably how humans
wound up being such a collectively destructive force.

To be sure, not all relationships that happen in nature are
sweet. There's plenty of competition, predation, parasitism –
the parts humans have focused on most since we internalized

"survival of the fittest" as the key evolutionary take-away. But there's also commensalism, relationships that really help one species and don't cost the other much, and mutualism, the win-win relationships of the natural world. Within each of these categories, there is a lot of variety, too. Out in the wild, death is visible everywhere, but there is also decomposition – breakdown enables new life. We don't have to model ourselves after everything we find in nature, but we do better when we are aware of what is outside of the spaces we made to shelter ourselves.

Through immersion in nature – and with appreciation of its myriad creative expressions, unknowable secrets, and delicate balances – it is possible to develop a more ecocentric and less people- or techno-centric worldview. We start to become less bullish about the chances that science and technology alone will allow us to evade ecological collapse; wary of centralized and expert-led decision making; and more intrigued by innovations that are low intensity, people-oriented, sustainable, democratic, and do not mandate participation in a global market system.[174] As we apply these insights to food and farming, we start to take seriously a kind of agriculture that recycles materials and runs on contemporary sunlight, just like an ecosystem. We not only learn from and emulate some of what we find in nature, but we develop a deep and surpassing appreciation that erodes our anthropocentric attitudes and takes us deeper into ecological consciousness and ethics. Eventually, we realize what deep ecology proponent Arne Næss wishes more humans would understand – that "the well-being and flourishing of human and non-human life on Earth have value in themselves [...] independent of the usefulness of the non-human world for human purposes."[175] In short, we fall in love with the whole of the world, not just with the parts that we've figured out how to use.

Building or deepening a relationship with nature is something many of us have to work at because our upbringings took place largely indoors. No judgment here. Nicole, who often quips that she was raised in restaurants and shopping malls, was an adult when she went on her first hike. She now lives in the woods, but doesn't yet know the names of many plants, animals and fungi living with her. Every walk from her cabin to the road is a chance to start or deepen a relationship with life in a different form, to have her curiosity piqued, and to learn more through quiet observation and good old fashioned research. This is part of how Nicole, a descendant of Italian and Irish immigrants responds to Robin Wall Kimmerer's invitation to become naturalized to place. Robin, a Potowatomi woman, offers settlers the option of learning to live "as if this is the land that feeds you, as if these are the streams from which you drink, that build your body and fill your spirit." The naturalization process doesn't end with a connection between self and place, though. It also requires knowing that the land, not just your person, bridges your ancestors and your children, and that the same ground matters to your children's futures. "To become naturalized is... to take care of the land as if our lives and the lives of all our relatives depend on it. Because they do."

When future generations tell the story of what got us out of the mess we have made of the food system, some themes will emerge. Future students will analyze those themes in their research papers just as we wrote papers on the New Deal or the fall of the Berlin Wall. They will say that we learned from our mistakes, regrouped, and changed the trajectory. We realized that our changes had to be *cosmolocal* – they had to freely and openly exchange knowledge but be more discerning about how we traded materials. We practiced *connected knowing*, building bridges between people, cultures, organizations, and countries, finding ways to humanize each other. We understood deeply the need for communities to pursue change in their own way, even while the goals were universal (*targeted universalism*) and we trusted what they knew about where and how they live (*ground truthing*). We not only gave back to each other and the Earth; we also gave forward to the future in *universal reciprocity*. We allowed ourselves to find and really feel *reverence and pleasure* with food and in our relationships. Divesting from perfectionism stopped us from fighting each other, from eviscerating ourselves. A little *humility* brought back *respect*. And throughout all of our successes, we saw our very human selves as a *part of nature*, not apart from or in charge of it. From a place of membership and belonging, we were able to learn from and defer to nature's patterns and wisdom, allowing ourselves to be guided by it even as we use our intellect and reason to do the really cool things that humans are capable of doing.

Life lived through these principles has the potential to keep us from ending up where we are headed. As more and more people make these changes, they become stronger and stronger signals of an emergent future.

Chapter 5

Emergent Examples

Complex patterns and systems emerge out of many, many relatively simple interactions. The way those interactions unfold are influenced by what we are calling culture. So if we want to shape change, we can either insist upon and enforce different interactions in the system or we can alter the culture and its influences and watch how behaviors, interactions, and even relationships begin to re-pattern. The former is familiar – we all know a decree or directive when we hear one. The latter can be described as emergent because we don't know what's going to happen to the patterns as they change so we are following the signals we receive and shaping change as we go.

Humans often stare with wild wonder when we witness emergence in non-human communities. If you've ever witnessed a murmuration of starlings move across the sky or a school of herring writhe and redirect, you've seen emergence in action. These are examples of thousands or even millions of individual organisms behaving in ways that are so attuned to each other they appear as a single superorganism. If we could view our own species from the same kind of remove, we might see similar patterns and behaviors of emergent and concerted action.

One of our beloved thinkers, Bayo Akomolafe, talks about emergence and activism "a notion of making sanctuary." He describes emergence as "a matter of irruptions and eruptions, breakthroughs, cracks, flashes, fissures, fault lines, discontinuities, blasts, splits, rifts, ruptures, seismic shifts, world-ending openings, miracles, strange encounters, and the yawning maw of a monster." For Bayo, emergence is a way of describing the "flows and possibilities that proceed from the moment when things no longer fit."[176]

When we work in systems, this kind of change is called emergent strategy. Emergent strategy, as with everything in this book, comes to us from a diverse set of theorists and activists. Henry Mintzberg, a professor at McGill University and Canadian academic who teaches and researches business strategy coined the phrase "emergent strategy" in 1985, to describe an alluring alternative to the top-down, directive approach to getting things done that was, and still is, common in the corporate world. His view was that strategy (how we get things done) emerges over time as our intentions collide with and change based on the realities we run into. These realities are not stable either, so we need to pay attention to the patterns that emerge and are realized over time to give us actions, behaviors, ideas, and plans where learning is the practice and change is the constant.

These groundbreaking ideas were picked up by Margaret Wheatley, a writer and facilitator on change and leadership. She ran with them, creating theories of change that are relational, human, and bridging. She says, "the world does not change one person at a time. It changes as networks of relationships form among people who discover they have a common cause and vision of what's possible... Through these relationships, we will develop the new knowledge, practices, courage, and commitment that leads to broad-based change."[177]

Activist adrienne maree brown picked up on these ideas, intersected them with the thinking of Grace Lee Boggs (a legend in the civil rights, labor, feminist, and environmental movements), and infused it with all the characteristics of emergence that are found in nature. The way that she remixed these ideas in her book titled *Emergent Strategy* struck a chord with social and racial justice activists, who helped to reinsert the concept of emergence in all the spaces they want to change – including the business world. A concept that resonates with both grassroots activists and counter-cultural CEOs might be one worth paying attention to. We suspect emergence feels so irresistible because when we tune into the way things happen in nature, we perceive emergence all around us. It is yet another reminder that we are a part of the natural world – and we can start acting like we belong in a wide community of life again.

Emergence can be used to forecast the future, at least enough for us to want to use it when we look at human behavior in complexity. Historian and futurist David J. Staley explains that "A complex adaptive system is an open system, one in which the individual parts interact with each other in such a complex manner that the overall behavior of the system cannot be determined. Indeed, the interaction of the parts often creates 'emergent behaviors' not exhibited by the individual parts themselves. There are a variety of complex adaptive systems in nature; in the realm of human affairs, complex adaptive systems are the norm. When someone says they want to know the future of something, what they're really saying is that they want to know the state or behavior – especially the emergent behaviors – of a complex adaptive system at some point in future."[178] It is those emergent behaviors we want to look at – and for us the focus is on how emergence works in nature.

Emergent strategy encourages us to look to the natural world to see how signals are shared within and between species – how bees swarm, how trees share information through root systems, how mycelium spread and behave, how ants move through obstacles. It also invites us to appreciate how complex forms in nature, including in our bodies, emerge from repetition of the same moves, branching and spiraling. These two forms create the fractal networks in trees, branches and waterways, neural structures and lung tissue, galaxies, hurricanes and the double helix of our DNA.

You don't even have to go outside to witness emergence in nature. If you like fermented foods – kraut and kimchee, yogurt and cheese, sourdough bread and beer – you can find examples of emergence and its transformative properties right in your kitchen. In the absence of oxygen, beneficial yeasts, bacteria and molds feast; they convert sugars into acids and alcohols and process proteins into amino acids and peptides.

While accurate and helpful to those whose countertops are not cluttered with bubbling jars and crocks, this simple description leaves all the magic out. A tiny but lively community of beneficial microbes emerges within hours. As time passes, these unseeable organisms live their best lives – eating, belching, and reproducing. In doing so, they also acidify the environment enabling foods to last longer, produce health-supporting antioxidants and enzymes, break down anti-nutrients, and generally make the resulting ferments more nutritious and strangely delicious. Though all ferments rely on the same basic biological concepts, no two kinds or even batches, are entirely alike. This is about as small as community and emergence gets.

Fermentation revivalist Sandor Katz likens what happens in a crock of kraut to the cultural ferment that allows change to emerge. "Metaphorical fermentation, the bubbliness and excitement of ideas whether in the single person's mind or in collective expression stems from the uniqueness of people: genetic difference layered upon family dynamics, culture, education, socioeconomic class, historical circumstances, and much more. Though all humans are related and share certain commonalities, we are also incredibly diverse and ultimately each of us is unique. It is this diversity of perspectives that makes metaphorical fermentation inevitable."[179]

Mara King, our personal fermentation mentor makes the connection for us between the jars on our counter and this book. While talking to Michelle about fermentation and food systems she dropped this wisdom: "Fermentation makes you ask 'What's the container?'" By container, Mara means a metaphor for both business practices and lifeways. "When you're fermenting, you're not thinking about making the lactobacillus do its work.

They do their own work. But you'll only get to the goal you desire if you create the right container and conditions for them to do that work. If the container is set up and filled correctly – anaerobic, with the right nutrients – then you just leave it up to everyone in the container to do their thing, you end up with something you want."

Mara counsels us to keep this in mind as we work in the food system. Focus less on trying to control all of the individual things that are happening and more on creating a healthy environment where things can take place. For us, that is emergence and culture change at its best. Mara takes it further though. "You can broaden this – we are, all of us, in a container – Planet Earth. Things had been doing great until we messed up the container. Now, we've got rot because we let the world run amok and forgot to make sure we protected our container."

Emerging Agrelationality

We know that to truly experience emergence we need to slow down and pay attention. Bayo Akomolafe also says "The times are urgent. We must slow down. The times are urgent! We must slow down. The times are urgent. We must slow down."[180]

In this final chapter, we share examples of emergent shifts brought about by those that cherish relationships and treat them with care. Slowing down to learn from example helps us appreciate that we are part of a growing community of change. The good news is there are people, communities, organizations, and approaches that demonstrate to us that change is possible. There are moments, places, and people where the change we are working towards comes to life. Even in the midst of extractive capitalism, we can open up liberatory possibilities and shape change on farms, in our communities, through the law, with our businesses, via education, and by how we choose to eat. Relational transformation takes many forms.

Further, drawing connections among and between relational experiments and movements helps us strengthen the kind of connected knowing we need for change. One of our most beloved thinkers, Ruth Wilson Gilmore, a liberatory geographer and abolitionist, has given us a way to think about the kind of connections that amount to "relational transformation." She says: "Solidarity is something that's made and remade and remade and remade. It never just is. I think of that in terms of radical dependency. That we come absolutely to depend on each other. And so solidarity, and this radical dependency that I keep thinking about and keep seeing everywhere, is about life and living and living together and living together in rather beautiful ways. And it's possible. It's really possible. And not in a romanticized way. In a material, deliberate, consciousness exploding kind of way. It's possible."[181]

Before we go to the solution, we want to myth bust. Independence, especially but not exclusively financial independence, is a myth. If COVID-19 taught us nothing else, it highlighted that we are all connected. Back when Michelle was in elementary school, her Jewish day camp had all the campers hold hands and sing a song about how wonderful the world would be if we were all connected. Fast forward 45 years and we now know exactly what that is like. We have seen the havoc it can wreak, but there are also benefits. So, as Shaun Chamberlin, who you met in Chapter Three explains, financial independence is not only a myth but one of our most dangerous ones. First, it sets you up to be a winner or a loser, competing and using each other for personal gain. But it also just isn't true. Even billionaires live in a house someone built and eat food someone grew and wear clothes someone made. Paradigm-shifting public scholar Charles Eisenstein lays it bare: "Financial security is not true independence, but merely dependence on strangers, who will only do the things necessary for your survival if you pay them."[182]

Once we admit that financial independence is a pernicious myth, we've also got to give the same treatment to "food independence." Resisting exploitative agricapitalist food systems by attempting to become "food independent" and grow everything yourself is not just difficult, self-defeating, and isolating – it can quickly trigger the same king of stockpiling and hoarding tendencies of doomsday preppers who respond to collapse by building themselves fortresses stocked with years of provisions. Such "independence," whether stored in charming mason jars or buckets of powdered food with a century-long shelf-life is a false idol. If you recognize and even revere the lives, agency, and kinship of plants, animals, and microbes, food always reveals the truth of interdependence. This alone is reason enough to recognize that relational is the right paradigm.

Agrelationality can liberate us. It can free us from chains we don't even know we are bound by. It prizes and pursues a form of collective liberation that follows the unashamed embrace of interdependence. Liberation of the people who work in the food system, the land, our bodies, and our minds. In its depths, relationality has the potential to recompose and recast our humanity, allowing us to reclaim our rightful role as part of – not apart from – nature. But before we plunge into the depths, we must (re)learn how to swim in the shallows, and sometimes we will retreat to the safety of the shore.

What follows are stories that splash and say: *Come on in, the water is fine.* You can trust this message because we are connected to each of the stories – our own collaborations with communities, businesses that drew us in as they put their values into practice, and an example from another country that is richly informing work we're plotting next. In other words, these are the emergent signals in our world that show us the patterns that could be. This is a bit of how we live together with our extended communities (and networks of change shapers) in rather beautiful ways. None of these examples are things done the easy way – each took a lot of creative, deliberate and sustained effort. All were worth it.

Agroecology: Science, Practice, and Social Movement

An authentically relational approach to agriculture already exists and is pushing back against the frontiers of extractive agribusiness. Agroecology took shape as a movement during the late 1970s in Latin America during a period when the region was reeling from trade liberalization conditions attached to loans from the International Monetary Fund. This opened the region to foreign profiteering – large transnational corporations swooped in to grab large swathes of land and act in ways that distorted local markets. Reeling from displacement and fierce competition, many small farmers – those whose land uses were informed by generations of cultural and biological evolution in their homelands – formed cooperatives and social movements. They exchanged knowledge and practices that made good use of local resources and were informed by the relationships they observed in natural ecosystems. Through reliance on polycultures (as opposed to monocultures), rejection of synthetic fertilizers, minimal machinery and attention to successional stages in planting, these farmers were able to support good crop yields, maintain ecological balance in and around cultivated lands, and avoid dependence on external inputs and debt-based entanglements with agrichemical companies.

Agroecology takes shape as a three-strand braid that plaits science with a set of farming practices and a social movement.[183] It is rooted in and evinces deep respect for the ecological orientation of indigenous and small-holder agriculture. Agroecology dignifies and elevates farmers' own knowledge; it does not approach the humans who tend the land as if they are deficient or in need of saving. Agroecologists favor bottom-up approaches to agricultural research and development that center local people, their knowledge, and what their local environs can provide. They also believe that change happens by spreading knowledge and power via relational exchange and in communities of practice. By offering a way to farm as part of nature, resetting the "culture" part of agriculture, and relating stories of resistance, agroecology offers a stable foundation for relational food systems.

Though agroecology remains less well known in the United States, where a focus on developing premium markets has shaped and selected "certified organic" as the challenger to synthetic agriculture – its relational orientation has enabled it to grow into a powerful movement in the southern hemisphere. Nevertheless, you can find vibrant agroecosystems – communities of plants and animals interacting with the land that is tended by people – dotted across North America – including on a vibrant acre of land in the Chaffee Park neighborhood of Denver, Colorado, known as Sister Gardens. The gardens are largely terraced – an ancient regenerative practice evident in places as diverse as the Hanging Gardens of Babylon and Machu Picchu in the Incan Empire. Ancestors in many places recognized that growing plants on stepped terrain captures nutrients at different levels of run off, decreases erosion, prevents nutrient loss and preserves water quality. Fruit trees, berry bushes, medicinal and insectary perennials are also grown near annual beds allowing beneficial relationships to form among the plants and their pollinators.

Sister Gardens manifests the vision and values of Frontline Farming, a farmer advocacy and food justice organization on the Front Range that operates three agroecological urban farms, a CSA, a BIPOC Farmer Apprenticeship Program, a research Center for Food Justice and Healthy Communities, and countless community education workshops. It was designed and tended by BIPOC and immigrant farmers who take their obligations to both land and culture seriously and know that both are the foundation of community and real wealth. While some of the terraces feature plantings that one might see on any urban farm in North America, three of them are based on distinct foodways.

With terraces for cultivating foods and foodways from Africa, the Middle East, and indigenous peoples of the Four Corners bio-region. Sister Gardens is, at once, an agroecosystem, a working farm that increases community food security, and a site of liberatory diasporic connection. Sister Gardens is also an important site for Frontline Farming's seed saving work, which focuses on both preserving and regionally adapting seeds that evolved in other places so they may thrive in a new environment. It does the same for people, too.

Frontline Farming's co-founding Executive Director and Head Farmer, Fatuma Emmad, speaks of the power of these three terraces: "One of the ways that we practice liberation is by telling the stories of the practices and foods that informed us and actually create the American tapestry in terms of foodways. So, it's not only about food but the cultures, and the ways that we prepare those foods, the stories behind them, the ways that people took to cultivating those things and the reasons why."

Fatuma, the child of immigrants from Yemen and Ethiopia, was born in Denver, Colorado. At age nine, she moved to Ethiopia and spent much of her childhood traveling between the U.S. and Ethiopia. Living in two countries sparked Fatuma's appreciation for the relationships between food, culture, identity, and belonging. It also prompted an early interest in macroeconomics and geopolitics – as she wondered about the forces that shaped a world system in which certain countries were historically food insecure while others were not. Fatuma trained and worked as a political scientist, with a sharp focus on policy issues that impacted marginalized farming communities, including the history of colonization in East Africa and imposition of "green revolution" technologies and genetically modified seeds across Sub-Saharan Africa.

Delving deeper into the political economy of agriculture, she became an ardent advocate for seed saving, preserving communities' rights to indigenous grains, and other forms of resistance to productivist single-solutions by the world's land caretakers. Determined to advance food sovereignty by embodying it and modeling more nuanced ways of farming, Fatuma obtained an agro-ecology certification from the University of California, Santa Cruz. But at least as important to her formation as a farmer were the lessons she learned from her elders, the close attention she paid to the work of traditional scientists, and the inspiration she takes from the women who care for the land on small farms across the world.

At its founding, Frontline Farming had no funding or investors, but it had the most important thing: a small group of people who genuinely ask how to be in right relationship with one another and the land, who dream of collective shifts, and who believe that, even in the United States, which is founded on oppression of BIPOC communities, it is possible to bring about change. When Fatuma, along with co-founders, Damien Thompson and JaSon Auguste, established Frontline Farming, they were clear and purposeful about establishing the farm and organization as part of the surrounding communities. "We are the communities we serve," she says, noting that Frontline's farms feed its farmers and provide wages that enable them to attain economic sustainability while also making food and relationship with the land available to neighbors. "As people of color who offer our labor to the land, we are visible representations of the strength and beauty of farming. When people see us, they believe that growing food is possible, accessible, and uplifting. Our relationships with each other and with the land offer other stories about BIPOC experiences in agriculture, challenging single-stories of oppression and replacing them with tangible evidence of our inherent liberation."

Cross-pollination: Agroecology and Abolition

Compared to industrial agriculture, agroecology is already radical and relational. But during 2020's reckoning with two viruses – COVID-19 and racism – environmental scientist Maywa Montenegro de Wit came to realize that agroecologists had a lot to learn from abolitionist movements – especially as they face ever stronger opposition from and co-opting by the agricapitalists. In a lengthy piece of relational scholarship, Maywa offers many connected insights from abolitionists (including Ruth Wilson Gilmore), which we distill and convey here.

First, the foundational structures organizing social life can be changed. Roundly rejecting the foundational (extractive, agricapitalist) structures of the food system will enable us to re-make them in life-affirming ways. We can take heart that the structures we see in the food system are not as solid, natural, or unchangeable as it serves neoliberal capitalism to make them seem.

Abolition is not merely a negative strategy. Ruth Wilson Gilmore says, "Abolition is about presence, not absence. It's about building life-affirming institutions." We are creating not destroying – this is true in abolition, agroecology, and agrelational moves of all sorts.

Reform is not enough. We know from our critical theory colleagues that reform always brings retrenchment.[184] Aim to transform, not reform the system.

It's important to spar and work out our differences. The struggle to survive also happens inside movements and communities and we all have a different view of what the future should look like.

Struggles always take us back to the land. Read this as shorthand for: Food system change will change everything because food always bridges us back to the land and into webs of interconnection from which we cannot extract ourselves.[185]

Though rewarding, the work of abolition and new creation is hard. Farming, even when it is a labor of love, isn't easy. The prevailing insistence that growing food should be as easy as possible is, in fact, part of what makes extractive, transactional, and objectifying approaches more widely appealing and accepted than relational, agroecological ones.

Relational values, even when they are deeply held, can also challenge an organization in practice. Despite disagreements and friction, Frontline Farming persists because its core team has a diverse set of skills, strong desire to use those skills in service of the community, and a belief that other ways of being together are possible. "We do not believe in hierarchies of knowledge and we do not expect perfection of ourselves or others. This allows us to uplift and rely on the strengths our communities already have – to work with what is present already. When things get tough, we return our focus to the land and to our commitments there. When we put those relationships first and use them to grow nourishment for our communities, what matters most rises up."

Going the Last Mile – Id Est Hospitality

Our friend Mara King landed a pretty rad gig as the Director of Fermentation for Id Est Hospitality, a restaurant group responsible for some of the most delicious and innovative food in Denver and Boulder, Colorado. "There's enough fermentation happening across four restaurants to merit a director?" we asked, more in awe than in disbelief. Our questions, by text mind you, continued: "Is this one of those jobs that is actually really common but people don't know about it unless they hang out back-of-the-house?" "Not really," said Mara, "I only know of three others – and one of them is at Noma." We already knew she was a total badass, but this took it to another level. Noma, for the uninitiated, is at the top of the restaurant world in every way from price to ideas to experience. "There should be more of us," she asserted. As lovers of ferments, we didn't need to be persuaded. "But not just because fermentation brings the flavor. Because cultured foods are an amazing way to change restaurant culture." We needed to know more...

Michelle already knew that Id Est was special. Basta, one of their restaurants in Boulder, is her favorite local spot. Moreover, Michelle met one of their chefs at Grain School, a place where all things about growing and cooking with grain are celebrated. The longer she talked to him about the role the restaurants he worked at were playing in rebuilding local grain economies, the clearer it became that something gutsy was going on. Kelly Whitaker the owner and force of nature who runs Id Est, takes chances. He cares a whole lot about the people he works with and he makes space for them to be creative and relational. He's managed to build an incredibly successful business in an industry where margins are tight. Restaurants – especially higher end ones – are notorious for their pressure cooker cultures and male chauvinism. While they may not appear as obviously extractive as a feedlot or meat processing plant, the way that many restaurants relate to food is akin to the way a magnate might relate to his trophy wife, which is to say that food is simultaneously put on a pedestal, but not deeply respected. But at Basta – and at Wolf's Tailor, Bruto, and Dry Storage (their grain mill and cafe) – food is revered and so are the people who work with it and the customers who return for truly memorable meals.

Michelle talked to Kelly and Mara to learn more about what they were up to, which was a geek-fest for Michelle, kind of like talking to a movie star while trying not to act like a dork. We wanted to know what differentiated Kelly's approach from that of other restaurateurs. His answer came quick: convenience. Others put it first and count on it to save the bottom line. In cutting costs and corners, they undermine their communities, diners, and the world. By contrast, Kelly aspires to three things in his restaurants: sustainability, viability, and thriveability. And, whenever he experiments with something new – whether it is a sourcing strategy, a practice, design, or recipe – he assesses how well it is advancing and balancing those aims.

For example, Id Est started getting some amazing results when they stopped stressing over food costs and started teaching their chefs how to reduce food waste. Kelly was interested in disrupting the relationship between food waste, the climate crisis, and food insecurity. While no local restaurant can solve global food waste on its own, it can catalyze a culture shift that has effects well beyond their own balance sheet.

Kelly is not your typical activist chef. He's too much the realist and business savant – to keep doing what he does in the economy that exists, he has to act as though the bottom line matters, because it does. He is determined to succeed – not at all costs but by doing things right. He told us that he took on food waste as a way to deal with the operating expenses of a restaurant. It was a gamble that paid off: costs to run his restaurants went down by 10 percent once he started focusing on how to make the most of every morsel. What's more, Kelly did it without buying into expensive systems for tracking food costs or by making his chefs' lives harder. Kelly knew his audience – chefs – don't light up over costs or metrics, but they sure are interested in relationship, location, taste, farming practices and what they add to flavor, texture, and experience. In other words, chefs shouldn't be accountants. They want to make great food. Kelly says "we gave our chefs permission to get the ingredients to make the food they wanted to make. Sure you can buy onions from a bulk place, but you could also get them from a local farm. They taste better and make the food incredible, and we make sure there is no waste from them."

It is easy enough, even for a home cook, to use all of an onion. Simply make sure your trim practices are on point and use the ends and skins to make stock. But Kelly and his crew take this approach further. The most inspiring example he offered involved a whole fish. As he appraises and appreciates the silvery body that once swam the ocean, Kelly asks, "How could I utilize it throughout the menu?" He closes his eyes and shows us the fish gliding through the kitchen. First, he cuts the collar and roasts it in a hot oven. Next, the belly gets grilled over charcoal. Then, the bones are boiled with vegetable peelings, onion ends, and herb stems to make stock. But they don't stop there. Next, they scrape those bones to make a noodle that gets served in the soup. One fish, four dishes.

The same kind of thing happens with bread. At Dry Storage, their bakery and grain mill, there's often leftover bread. They use some of that bread to make kvass, a fermented drink that has a place of pride on their menu. And another portion of it as a base for fermented gochujang, which then gets used as an ingredient elsewhere.

Loaves and fishes multiply. Hmmmm... where have we heard that before?

Across his restaurants, Kelly now needs the extra that he might once have abhorred as evidence of poor menu and budget management to make the very ingredients that make the food special. "So is it even 'waste'? There's no waste. There's just ingredients when you think about it right," Kelly muses. Waste, like weeds, is a social construct. Food becomes waste when we stop seeing its potential.

That is where Mara King comes into the story. As Kelly and Mara got to working together, Kelly thought Mara's work would be about preserving food to avoid waste. But before long, he realized what they were actually talking about was flavor – big, nuanced, and evolving. They agreed that food should be complex, it should take time, and it should be delicious. Mara, for her part, realized Kelly's unwillingness to follow the crowd or lean on conventional wisdom had something like shape-shifting implications. Approaching the "problem" of food waste from a different angle, they were able to see that it wasn't a problem after all – it was an opportunity in disguise.

Mara brought her well-researched and deeply practiced fermentation skills to Kelly's totally modern business – and the outcomes were unexpected and striking. For example, they found that when you make more of your own ingredients and buy from local farmers, supply chain issues are just not that big a deal. When you free chefs up to buy more expensive local ingredients – but make sure they make the most of them – you have more control and more access to what you want. You can get to know farmers in your area, understand that, say, buckwheat would be good for the land and soil in your region, and design a menu that celebrates it, fill your restaurant, and grow your acclaim in the food world, which is exactly what they did.

When we spoke with Kelly and Mara, they had just wrapped a shoot of his new menu – one that took seven months to develop – for *Art Culinaire Magazine*. For the article, Kelly shared his processes, his spaces, his ideas, his recipes – what other chefs might call their secrets. Why so unguarded? Because "it's a battle against a race to the bottom," Kelly tells us. "At the end of the day, we're trying to open source information as much as possible... We worked with all the collaborators we could work with, and then gave them everything to print in the magazine." Kelly knows this means in another four months, everyone's going to try all the recipes, theories, and practices. He's not threatened by that – he thinks it is beautiful and overdue. Sounds a lot like cosmolocalism, right? Instead of trying to maximize his profits by maintaining a monopoly on his ideas, Kelly is excited that every major chef in the world will be able to see what his team is doing and adapt it for their place and context.

As collapse accelerates, Kelly observes that "we are on the clock now more than ever. We've got problems we can only solve together." He's acting as proof of concept for collaboration, relationship, reverence, cosmolocalism, and he makes it all taste good. Kelly wants others to be thinking, as he does, about designing their kitchens, dining areas, recipes, and menus with flexibility in mind. Such design allows for creative and conserving in-house valorization of ingredients.

He's not looking for accolades or acolytes. Even though he owns some of the coolest places in Denver and Boulder, Kelly jokes that he hates restaurant swag. You won't catch him in a branded T-shirt or baseball cap. What he wants is "mind swag" he wants someone to walk away with an experience that stays with them, a last mile connection to the food, inspired by the ideas that created it. He wants diners to make different choices out in the world and not even know why, but we know, because they received some free mind swag with their meal.

"Without flavor," Kelly explains, "it's hard to take these ideas the last mile." In the logistics and distribution parlance, the last mile refers to the very last step of the delivery process in which a parcel moves from a transportation hub to its final destination. This is the most critical and expensive step in the delivery process – and the one that requires the most custom path. It is also where we often lose or waste food – in that final leg of the journey between farm and face. For Kelly, the last mile has a different valence; he uses the term to mean the set of steps one must take to move from a great idea to a great business. Both reviving local food through farmer collaborations and transfiguring food waste through culinary craft are sizable strides, but neither will traverse the last mile and make your restaurant the place to be. For that, you need several dashes of cool: the mood lighting, the right songs, the hipster aprons, the bartender who remembers your drink order, a moment of visual delight right before gustatory gratification. Yes, this is a recipe for pleasure. But it is also a way to make the ideas go viral – ideas that might change how some of us, especially those with resources to spare, think about and take a relationship to food.

Project Protect Food Systems Workers

The story of Project Protect Food Systems Workers is about how individuals, communities, and eventually coalitions reach for and achieve basic rights, support, and recognition for their participation in our systems and economies. This is a story that takes place completely within extractive capitalism and highlights that we can begin to make the changes we need now – economically, legislatively, and systematically.

Project Protect Food Systems Workers is just a group of people who stood up to systems of oppression by prioritizing relationships and holding fast to the aim of redressing historical wrongs. We focused on creating what the anarchist activist Hakim Bey called a Temporary Autonomous Zone, or a place where we could experience the world with the rules of agricapitalism and supremacy suspended.[186] In other words, we got a glimpse of the relational future.

In the fear-filled and chaotic first weeks of the pandemic, when the country, and most of the economy, were "shut down," millions of workers categorized as essential saw no decrease in the pace of their work – and substantial increases in its peril. The designation of agriculture and food production workers as essential exposed "a cruel paradox: everyone relies on food system workers to meet their basic needs for sustenance in times of calm and crisis, but many food system workers do not have secure livelihoods and exist on the margins of society."[187]

The coexistent essential worker designation and the lack of concern for worker safety rendered an exploited underclass more vulnerable – and it leveraged their very bodies so that the rest of us could eat. Their vulnerability generates great economic benefit for the owners of farms, companies, and whole industries whose business models rely upon worker exploitation.

Recognizing these particular vulnerabilities – and noticing that groups aiming to address pandemic disruptions to Colorado's food system seemed insufficiently attentive to the needs of workers – a loosely organized Colorado Food System Workers Rapid Response Team spun out of other efforts and into its own Zoom meetings. Early meetings drew dozens of people from across the state, each of whom logged on to share community needs or offer expertise and resources. The conversations made space for many perspectives and allowed us to practice connected knowing and ground truthing. Each meeting began with a meditation and ended with a blessing, keeping reverence alive in the difficult conversations. The organizers and attendees of these meetings were troubled by their shared recognition that "[f]ederal relief directed toward the agriculture sector prioritized the needs of business owners, but largely ignored the specific vulnerabilities and needs of Food System Workers."[188]

Before long, this group of "immigrants, farmers, scholars, activists, unions, and workers across Colorado working to identify, elevate and address the needs of the people who contribute their labor to all parts of the food system,"[189] gave itself a more compelling name: Project Protect Food Systems Workers (PPFSW). It was our belief that food systems workers are always essential but that their rights, health, needs, and interests had been systematically ignored for far too long because their vulnerability and structurally racist marginalization was a boon to extractive agricapitalism. Inattention to the plight and the health of food system workers is unsurprising but deeply problematic.

Based on the information we were getting from the workers themselves, we realized that PPE and COVID-19 information was the first need to meet. So, we started gathering donations, disseminating information, and working on distribution. Then, as the pandemic continued, workers and their families shared that they were experiencing food insecurity; we began delivering food. Warm weather gear followed, and a loose system of affiliated people and organizations became a community. Our strategy was not top down or dictated by grant funding but emergent based on the needs of the workers, the strange permutations of pandemic life, and the available resources.

What emerged first were a set of guiding principles followed by action.

The only requirement of any individual or organization wishing to attend our meetings, align with, or contribute to our work has been a willingness to uphold and be guided by these principles. As such, this foundational document has influenced all aspects of our advocacy, actions, structure, relationships, and coalition building.

1. *Essential, Not Expendable*
   A contradiction of capitalism is the existence of people whose marginalization both economically and socially is essential to the proper functioning of the economy. To recognize another's humanity is to treat that person with dignity, regardless of legal status in a particular location. Access to jobs, education, housing and a healthy environment in which to live are foundational supports for essential workers in any economic system.

2. *No Justice, No Security*
   We know the security of any system only exists insofar as the individuals and communities supporting that system are themselves secure. As long as workers are vulnerable to coercive threats from employers and the state, the food system will not be secured.

3. *Protection of Workers & Environment Is Good Business*
   The food system will be secure when workers are owners, when they are well-paid and their families are well-fed and housed decently. The food system will be secure when farmworkers are known and respected as land stewards. The food system will be secure when animals meet their end in culturally appropriate ways that honor the relationship between humans and our animal relations.

4. *Equity in Risk and Opportunity*
   The essential but expendable paradigm reveals that some are called upon to potentially sacrifice their lives for the wellbeing of the economy. Essential workers should have access to greater opportunities in housing, education and healthcare equal to the proportion of risk (e.g., measured by death, dismemberment, chronic disease, shortened lifespan, etc.) that they endure for the sake of "our" economic system.

5. *Nurture Economies of Solidarity and Resilience*
   Vulnerable communities have long created economies that leverage local assets in historically rooted, culturally appropriate and mutually supportive ways. It is critical that these supportive networks are nurtured as they provide critical structures of resilience and resistance to communities that are marginalized in the current food system.

6. *Land based, People based*
   Our resilience is rooted in land and the capacities of people in our communities.

7. *We Elevate and Amplify (Essential) Worker Voices*
   None are liberated until all are liberated. We recognize every human being has the ability to work towards liberation and become self-sufficient by creating necessary systems. In a liberated society, every voice is lifted and every one of us is visible and our contributions are recognized.

   Spelling out these principles early in our organizational history proved invaluable – they provided shared purpose and expectations that we could return to as we navigated the challenges, conflicts, and trade-offs that inevitably arise in any change effort.

   As we felt our way through the Summer of 2020, its nation-wide reckoning with the violent and deadly consequences of structural racism, racial disparities in COVID-19 infections, deaths, and other harms, and continued instrumentalization of "essential workers," early brainstorms of a Promotora Network that could span the state turned into meetings with the Colorado Department of Public Health and Environment and proposals for funds. Likewise, aspirational musings about legislation that would make legendary farmworker rights' advocates Cesar Chavez and Dolores Huerta proud turned into draft provisions and conversations with potential legislative sponsors. Progress was possible not because we were the most experienced political operatives or organizers but because we held fast to a relational approach that emerged from and responded to the needs of the moment. Understanding both historical drivers and present harms, we knew that we had to undertake both projects – and that, while separate, each would energize and inform the other.

Creating the Promotora Network

Models for a Promotora network already existed and seemed like an obvious and culturally appropriate response.[190] In looking to such models and practices, we recognized that "in order to meaningfully increase health equity in our communities, community leaders of color must be at the table and involved in identifying the barriers and creating the solutions as well as being involved in decisions about activities that may affect their communities' environment and/or health."[191] Further, seeing that, when COVID-19 response in frontline communities isn't done in a culturally responsive way, it has immediate negative impacts and can contribute to future outbreaks and overall local community insecurity,[192] we sought to support a network of *promotores* – skilled and respected Latinx community members who work within their community to bring resources, advocacy and needed services.

The network was created to train and provide resources for a group of promotores across the state who are knowledgeable in legal, health and food-related issues that confront food systems workers in response to COVID-19.[193] PPFSW determined that our promotores would:

- support and work in tandem with Regional Labor and Employment Specialists,
- live in the geographic region where they work, and have connections to the farm/food worker communities therein. We envisioned a state-wide network of promotores who would:
- work in collaboration with agencies and members of the community to bring community voice to inform and influence decisions that impact their lives;
- provide community education around health, legal guidance, and available resources including personal protective equipment (PPE) supplies;
- provide support for community members who are experiencing additional vulnerabilities related to COVID-19; and
- provide support for community members who are Colorado residents as well as community members who are not residents but who are employed in the state or are required by public health officials to remain in Colorado as a result of COVID-19 exposure.

Before we could make this vision a reality, we needed to reverse the invisibilization of farmworkers. Our indefatigable data team, led by an early-career researcher Kassandra Neiss, took on the task of figuring out who the people laboring across Colorado's fields and ranges were, where they were, where they came from, what languages they spoke, what work they did at what times of year. Once we had mapped the Colorado farmworker population and assembled basic demographic information about them, we could connect directly and find out more about what they wanted. What little research there was on Colorado's farmworkers was premised on employers' opinions about workers – most of it did not involve actually interviewing the farmworkers themselves. So we perceived and responded to an unmet need for information.

We were committed to taking action grounded in the realities of farmworker lives and not on the perceptions or assumptions that usually drive toxic philanthropy. As the pandemic hit its height, two members with unique and pertinent skills and connections, Fatuma Emmad and Jenifer Rodriguez, began the work of weaving together a coalition of Promotoras across the state. Through interviews with outreach workers and trusted community members, Jenifer and Fatuma began to identify leaders across regions who had already been doing the work of outreach in different capacities, often unpaid.

They approached these communities from an asset-based perspective and with humility. This approach allowed an understanding, mutual recognition, and a small-scale state-wide cosmolocal structure and approach. As a result, these communities now recognize that there is so much that connects them despite the distances and differences in a large and varied state. They also appreciate that each community has unique assets to offer and needs to source help for.

Finally, the Promotoras don't just help agricultural workers deal with challenges, access resources, and redress wrongs. They also draw their communities together in ways that honor and celebrate culture in new contexts. For example, we held a *Día de Muertos* vigil and celebration to honor agricultural workers who died doing their work. The promotores are not all accustomed to the same celebrations so it was also a learning experience planning the event – with each person asking for the food, music, altars, and ways of doing the event that they were used to. By the time the event was starting, there were many cultures coming together to dance, sing, mourn, laugh, teach, and learn. The dancing, music, and sharing went on for hours in the cold November dusk outside a state office building creating warmth that kept us all there for hours. By building cultures that create joy and meaning even amidst mundane tasks or grinding challenges, the Promotoras open up the possibility for thriving in systems that do not have their communities' best interests at heart.

Passing Senate Bill 21-087 concerning Agricultural Workers Rights

The long history of labor exploitation in U.S. agriculture and the structural racism of its roots in the slave trade meant that many contemporary farmers and their well-resourced and organized industry associations saw little wrong with labor dynamics that keep a largely BIPOC and migrant workforce at the margins of society and the economy while demanding the performance of hard physical and manual labor in the unsheltered outdoors often in excess of 60 hours per week. Such had been the norm for so long that the business models of individual farms and agribusiness sub-sectors had become reliant on artificially and exploitatively low labor costs and safety standards. Indeed, in some ways, this arrangement is what made it possible for an American agricapitalism to extract maximum value from stolen indigenous lands while rewarding homesteaders (and later ever-larger farm operators) who spread across the continent and reinforced tenuous claims to large swathes of land by rendering it "productive." As a result, it is not surprising that (mostly white and landowning) farmers across Colorado clamored that they would "not be able to make any money" when they heard that PPFSW and its allies were working to rewrite the state's agricultural labor laws.

Having immersed ourselves in legal and movement history, we knew that the only way to rectify legal exclusions and agricultural exceptionalism was to create legislation. So, in Colorado, we needed to propose a bill and pass it – even if doing so would be akin to ascending the tallest peaks in the Rocky Mountain state barefoot. But if we didn't climb, the centuries-long legacy of racialized labor exploitation in agriculture would survive the pandemic.[194]

In February of 2021, Senator Jessie Danielson introduced Senate Bill 21-087, the Agricultural Workers' Rights' Bill, into the Colorado Senate. The Bill was co-sponsored by Representatives Karen McCormick and Yadira Caraveo in the House.

The process and the response from the farmers was an education in White Supremacy and its symbiotic relationship with extractive capitalism. With no compunction, opponents of the legislation expressed that denying the basic rights of workers in order to safeguard owner profit was completely reasonable.

Bear in mind, the bill was a basic rights bill, only bringing agricultural workers up to the lowest standard of rights other workers in the state enjoyed such as:

- Providing basic health and safety protections during the pandemic;
- Extending the right to organize to farmworkers;
- Ensuring that service providers like doctors have access to farmworkers in employer-provided housing;
- Ensuring fair pay of at least the minimum wage and overtime based on rules enacted by the Colorado Department of Labor and Employment;
- Mandating rest breaks and other protections against overwork, especially in extreme heat; and
- Providing protections against retaliation for farmworkers who speak out about mistreatment.

But, as the bill worked (climbed) through the legislature, Project Protect collaborated with allied organizations, especially Towards Justice and the Hispanic Affairs Project, to clear each hurdle and widen our coalition of advocates and activists. Additionally, though restricted from participating in direct legislative advocacy, the experienced staff of Colorado Legal Services Migrant Farm Worker Division brought both legal expertise and ground-truth to the public debate, offered persuasive testimony, and invaluable, trusted guidance to the drafters and sponsors. Each group within PPFSW and our coalition of SB-87 proponents played a part tailored to the goals of their community and the resources they had at their disposal. Many compromises were hashed out to clear various political blockades thrown up by legislative opponents and the Governor's office. While several of these were hard to swallow – especially those made late at night to overcome Republican blustering and endless cowboy fantasizing – when all was said and done, we won far more rights and protections than we had imagined possible in our first legislative effort. In a matter of months, we were able to legally guarantee farmworkers in Colorado fairer wages, a right to collective action and ability to form unions, protections against overwork and heat stress, a prohibition against the injurious short handled hoe and limitations on extensive stooped labor, ability to access key service providers and basic necessities, retaliation protections, and an official forum for public participation.

Belo Horizonte – The City That Ended Hunger

Belo Horizonte, the sixth largest city in Brazil, is now known as "the city that ended hunger." But things were not always that way. Brazil is a country with inequity in land ownership, economic development, and access to food, as well as sharp class divides and racial tensions. The country began to pay attention to hunger after World War II. However, the interventions they attempted had an all too familiar neoliberal capitalist bent and were premised upon its faulty assumptions: namely, that economic growth and export agriculture would increase access to food for the poorest people. For all the reasons you now know, it didn't work. Even though Brazil generally has enough arable land to feed its population and the economic wherewithal to import, people on the losing end of income inequity could not readily or reliably access food. Brazil also had the world's thirteenth highest level of income inequality (and more recently ranked seventeenth) – which tells us the country was not in a particularly special or advantageous position when it came to addressing hunger.

Once it became apparent that starvation worked faster than economic development, they turned to technocratic solutions and more nutrition research. Didn't work. They tried to change the system from the centralized government. Again, no dice. Brazilian philosophies that failed to address inequality and access policies made no headway. Left-leaning grassroots organizers pressed for change; amid a sweeping transition in systems of governance towards the end of the twentieth century, Brazil decentralized power and gave substantial authority to its municipalities – even more than delegated to the states.

Around that time, Belo Horizonte was particularly challenged: 40 percent of the city's population lived below the poverty line – malnourishment was rampant and children were dying as a result. The city used its new authority and financial resources, along with the fresh ideas like participatory equity, which came from the progressive movements, to go after hunger, once and for all. In 1993, Belo Horizonte declared that its citizens had a right to food and then established a municipal food secretariat to make good on the declaration.

Of course, they used data and technology appropriately to scope and explain the problems. But they also dug deeper – held interviews, talked to people and came up with a multifaceted plan that met populations where they were, addressing needs in ways that were culturally specific and met with enthusiasm. Targeted universalism and ground-truthing in action.

One of Belo Horizonte's most successful programs was to bring back the *Restaurante Popular*, an institution feeding 12,000 to 14,000 meals a day of food that customers ranked as excellent. The meals cost the same for everyone – regardless of need – and the cost is amazingly low. This low but equal price was a source of pride for the program and for the customers, who never had to deal with the stigma of paying a reduced or different price. Those unable to pay were slipped a *real* by a social worker and they paid for their meal, now 100 percent subsidized, like everyone else.

School meals followed suit, they were nutritionally balanced but designed to be tasty too. The principle of pleasure was extended even to school kids.

Where did the food come from? The city established a local "Family Farm Food Purchase Program." The municipality bought produce from local farmers directly, as much as they could provide, assuring a stable supply and manageable prices while helping the farmers earn a fair and sufficient income. There were also programs to provide local farmers more stability by allotting them spaces in local farm stands to sell their produce directly to the citizens. Again they cut out the profit motive of any middle man and they placed the farm stands fairly around the city so that there were no food apartheid zones.

To address further access gaps, they also created ABC markets. At these markets, named for *Alimentos a Baixo Custo* or "Food at Low Cost," affordable prices were mandated for 25 products that were most needed by families at risk of malnutrition. Beyond that, market owners could stock whatever they wanted and sell it at their own prices. What did the store owners get in return? Concessions on rent so they did not suffer any income loss by serving those in need.

There were numerous other programs that provided enriched flour, had farmer convoys supply fresh produce all over the city, brought food to community centers and retirement homes, and a myriad of other relational solutions that took into account the real lived experience of the people in the city.

The outcome was astounding. From a book on the suite of programs, these are the headline results:

- Child hospitalizations for malnutrition decreased by 60 percent;
- Mortality rates for children under five years old decreased by nearly the same amount;
- Infant mortality, for babies under a year old, fell by more than 70 percent;
- Hospitalization due to diabetes dropped by 33 percent;
- The Taquaril neighborhood, one of Belo Horizonte's poorest, saw infant mortality decrease rapidly right away: in 1993 it had twice the incidence of infant mortality as the city average; by 1997 it reached parity;
- Per capita household consumption of fruits and vegetables increased 25 percent between 1987 and 1997; Belo Horizonte went from sixth to first in consumption of green vegetables and eighth to second in consumption of fruits;
- An estimated 800,000 citizens interact each year with BH's programs – almost 40 percent of the population in 2003.

With that kind of success, you might wonder how they got the word out. Their main strategy was simple: word of mouth. Belo Horizonte relied on creating impactful programs and trusted that the people would relate the benefits to each other.[195]

By treating food as a right of citizenship before it can be seen as a source of profit, Belo Horizonte was able to meaningfully address a problem that has defied market and development solutions. Belo Horizonte wasn't afraid to address the failures of the market, link the interests of eaters and farmers, experiment with multiple interventions, and elevate the dignity of all involved. While we can't simply copy Belo Horizonte's programs and implement them in our own places, we can take inspiration from them, use our relational tools – like connected knowing, targeted universalism, and ground-truthing – and design a suite of strategies that will address hunger while rebuilding our local and regional food systems. As we take what we learned from the process of passing SB-21-087 and start directing our change-shaping energies to advocacy for collapse-aware agriculture and food policies in our own regions, the successes in Belo Horizonte provide guidance and inspiration for realizing a right to food.

Diaspora Spice Co.

There are already many food businesses making big moves toward relationality, leading with and through their values, and striving to balance ethical and financially sustainable operations. Whether they are local farms, craftspeople and small business owners, or niche players trying to upset an extractive industry, we appreciate the entrepreneurs who *soulsearch* before they *profitseek* – and we know they haven't set up shop on Easy Street. By now, you know that we love and support Josh, our coffee guy, for all the agrelational choices he makes. But he is not the only entrepreneur who has captured our hearts and stomachs. Here, we've chosen to highlight Diaspora Co. because they are doing the work of repair and regeneration in a part of the food system that has been inextricably and terribly tied up with the colonial project: the spice trade. They are also breaking binaries

175

and operating loudly from the relational paradigm in bright pink and orange branding – offering messages and imagery that won't easily be missed.

A few years ago, while trading recipes, Michelle and Nicole each tried to introduce the other to a new-ish, direct-to-consumer, single-origin spice company that we were becoming a little obsessed with. When Nicole wouldn't stop gushing about the way its young, queer, female, South Asian immigrant founder, Sana Javeri Kadri, was developing intentional supply relationships with smallholders in South Asia, Michelle hurried the conversation along. She already knew all this and wanted to focus on the fact that Nicole had not yet tried Diaspora Co.'s Aranya Black Pepper, which is so nuanced and flavorful that we now find our family members sneaking and snacking on peppercorns straight from the jar. How is Diaspora Co. putting "money, equity and power into the best regenerative spice farms across South Asia, and bring(ing) wildly delicious, hella potent flavors into your home cooking"? By departing entirely from the colonial conquest history of the spice trade and throwing the commodity model out of the window.

Four hundred-ish years after the colonial conquest of the Indian subcontinent, Sana Javeri Kadri realized that the spice trade was still dominated by imperially bad ideas. Ideas that left farmers with little to live on, passed profits between middlemen upwards of 10 times, and put jar after jar of flat, dusty spices in pantries around the world. Seeing an opportunity to decolonize and decommoditize the traditional supply chain, she hopped a plane back to her birthplace of Mumbai and spent the next seven months learning the terrain. "Forty-plus farm visits, endless un-answered phone calls, a squishy motorbike ride through a rice paddy, and one life-changing meeting with the good folks at the Indian Institute of Spices Research" later, the audacious 23-year-old started Diaspora Co. by "offering just one spice – Pragati

Turmeric – sourced from an equally young and idealistic farm partner, our now dear friend Mr. Prabhu Kasaraneni."

Five years later, Diaspora has built relationships with and opportunities for 150 farms across India and Sri Lanka and is able to offer 30 single-origin spices, so once a harvest sells out (and they do), there's no more until next season. On average, Diaspora Co. pays its farm partners four to six times the commodity price. Compare this to the 15 percent premium that most "fair trade" supply systems offer, and you can see why relational and direct trade models are better for smallholders. Diaspora Co. offers prices that amount to a living wage and position farmers to be community leaders and land stewards capable of creating resilience in places predicted to be most hard hit by climate chaos. This means that filling an online shopping cart with Diaspora Co. spices will set you back more than loading up at Walmart or Costco. But spices are not the kind of food we rely upon to evade starvation and there is really no legitimate reason to make them artificially cheap. Moreover, beyond the social mission and environmental benefits, Diaspora's spices are also of tremendous culinary value. They are so potent and nuanced that we use smaller amounts (as compared to commodity spices) and wind up with far more flavorful dishes. A true pleasure.

The company deliberately distinguishes its direct-trade model from typical commodity supply chains. In the commodity model, the chain of transitions and transactions is long: After a farmer produces a spice, it moves through auction houses, multiple traders, exporters, importers, one or more consumer product goods companies, and a retailer before making its way to a consumer's shopping cart. It typically takes five to ten years to get spices into kitchens. Crops from numerous farms are treated as fungible and mixed together at every stage. Quality has only aesthetic indicators, like color and size. Outside of possible organic certification, little attention is paid to how the spices were grown, which seed varieties they came from, and how they taste or smell. In this mode, farmers are not only price-takers, but they also have no incentive to distinguish their spices in terms of sensory appeal or sustainable production practices. In Diaspora Co.'s model, by contrast, spices are grown for flavor and potency using regenerative practices on multigenerational family farms. While it can take years to build a farm partnership, once harvested, spices move to kitchens within 6–12 months. The only players involved are the farmers, Diaspora Co., and community sourcing partners who add "an important layer of on the ground relationship building and quality control."

The company reportedly derives energy from the dynamic tension between its values and the priorities of agricapitalism and does some of its best work when it strides right into those contradictions. Baking social impact into its business model gives Diaspora Co. a way to drive change through its regular operations. To amplify impact beyond creating markets for premium spices, Diaspora Co. has recently established a Farm Worker Fund. Through it, the social and economic wellbeing of the 850-plus farmworkers from vulnerable migrant, Dalit, and tribal communities in South Asia can be safeguarded. To do this well, Diaspora has been surveying farmworkers across the subcontinent and honing programs in response, not unlike the Project Protect Promotora Network has done.

Diaspora Co.'s intentionality and authenticity are as pungent as its spices. Lots of companies talk about building community with its suppliers and customers, but more often than not, their words ring hollow. But we open every email Diaspora Co. sends, cook recipes from its website and actually learn a lot from its blog. We are even following them on Discord and learning from the conversations. After a harvest report landed in her inbox, Nicole once asked Michelle if she'd read the update on "our" turmeric farm – by which Nicole meant Mr. Kasaraneni's land in Andhra Pradesh. With that easy turn of phrase, we realized that Diaspora Co. had created as strong a set of community connections as any local CSAs we'd ever joined and loved – except they'd created mutual interests and empathy that stretched halfway across the world. On its website, Diaspora says that "[b]eing in this community is about connecting deeply with the culture and heritage of the regions that we source from, and about learning as we go. Complicating and deepening what 'Made in South Asia' means, and how we tell our own stories of freedom, struggle, and diaspora through food." The epitome of relationship through food and story – and enacted by a private company.

The difference may be that Diaspora Co. also identifies itself as a queer business.[196] The Diaspora Co. team didn't just start tossing this around as a trendy, counter-cultural label; they penned a ten-point Queer Business Manifesto, which speaks to how they hold the tensions between the transactional defaults of the business world and their relational values.

1. As we've learned from our Black trans and queer elders, queerness is rooted in liberation, while business is capitalism itself. We operate within and are acutely aware of the tension that arises from pairing these two words together.
2. Being queer isn't about your preferences or your sexuality, rather your willingness to defy what is seen as "normal" and embrace the possibilities of wild, magical, and radical ways of being.
3. We choose to be rooted in equity, empathy, and transparency.
4. *Business is inherently transactional, and we both benefit greatly from those transactions, and suffer from the entitlement they can generate. Mutual respect and healthy boundaries help us reprioritize relationships over transactions.*
5. Our business is a daily and intentional gathering of people. It means we take the time to connect and care

about everyone on the team as full people, with honesty, trust, mutual learning, and love.

6. Professionalism is rooted in white supremacy. We prioritize our own and collective comfort, we interact with care, and somehow, we still get shit done.

7. OUR EMAILS WILL ALWAYS HAVE EMOJIS, SMILEY FACES AND EXCLAMATION MARKS!!!:)

8. Nobody (not the CEO, not the customer, not your parent) is always right. We will fail and make mistakes every day; embracing those mistakes is how we learn new ways of doing.

9. THIS IS NOT A PHASE. We'll always be rooted in points 1–9 BUT we maintain the full creative license to grow and evolve.

10. We want the future to make us redundant. For the future to be so queer that this manifesto only serves as an archive of a different, transitional time.

Diaspora Co.'s staff steeped themselves in the wisdom of Audre Lorde when developing their manifesto: "The principal horror of any system which defines the good in terms of profit rather than in terms of human need, or which defines human need to the exclusion of the psychic and emotional components of that need – the principal horror of such a system is that it robs our work of its erotic value, its erotic power and life appeal and fulfillment. Such a system reduces work to a travesty of necessities, a duty by which we earn bread or oblivion for ourselves and those we love."[197] Based on how they've built their business to date, how they pledge to learn from past and future missteps, and how much desire and pleasure are packed into each of their spice jars, we'd say they've answered Audre Lorde's call.

EcoGather

For several years, Nicole taught food systems at Sterling College, a tiny school perched on a hilltop in Vermont's Northeast

Kingdom that has been a haven for people moved to care for a wounded world with nature-based wisdom and practical skills. When she began working with undergraduates, she always started by helping them realize that no one of them would be able to end environmental degradation, repair the cruel legacies of genocide and racism, or fix the food system on their own – but they could all be shiny, colorful parts of the change-mosaic they wanted to see in the world. She also inculcated a healthy skepticism about the notion that the ideologies and corporations that devastated the planet for profit would be the ones to foster restoration. To find purpose, belonging, and meaning in a changed and changing world, she and her colleagues focused on helping students come into right relationship with the land and our kin. Her students had the rare chance to bring their study of heady topics like systems, economics, policy, culture, ethics, and sovereignty to life by spending lots of time outdoors, working on the farm and in the kitchen to nourish their community, collecting and sharing stories, and trying to tend each other's hearts as carefully as they'd tend to new lambs and seedlings.

Without question, facilitated learning in such an embodied and deeply relational manner is transformative for both teacher and student. But when she lay awake at night, Nicole would often wonder if it was enough to reach so few students when so many people deserved to know about the breaking aspects of the agricapitalist food system and to build the skills that would allow bridging alternatives to take shape. E.F. Schumacher had certainly persuaded her that "Small is Beautiful." But was "small" enough in the twenty-first century?

Uncertainty prompted her to try teaching in a different program that was rapidly scaling up – but she quickly found her impact diluted as she stretched attention across too many students and operated in too rigid an institutional bureaucracy. David Fleming's system-scale rule gave her a way around the

Goldilocks problem at the heart of her teaching career: "Large-scale problems do not require large-scale solutions; they require small-scale solutions within a large-scale framework."[198] With the generous support from an anonymous foundation that accepts the reality of collapse, supports communities of practice, and sees emergence as nature's way of scaling, Nicole returned to Sterling to manifest EcoGather.

EcoGather takes the principles of cosmolocalism and applies them to education. The initiative aims to provide accessible online education that connects communities so they can cope with collapse and live into new ways of being together guided by ecological knowledge and relational ethics. The "eco" part of EcoGather is probably obvious; the "gather" part is a little less so, especially in the context of online learning. Here's the distinguishing feature: EcoGather fosters connections with aligned communities that want to learn from and transform our relationships with each other, the rest of the natural world, and life itself.

As she stepped into the role of directing EcoGather, Nicole determined that EcoGather resources – funds, as well as the time and skills of its personnel – would be shared with partner organizations to co-create online learning opportunities that connect holders of place-based knowledge to support agroecological transition, create relational food systems, and build community capacity for change. Before digging into the work, she formed or furthered relationships with each of our partner organizations – Frontline Farming, the Gross National Happiness Center Bhutan, the Maati Pani Asha Center in India, the Puerto Rico Science, Research and Technology Trust and Plenitud PR – and asked them to identify what they could contribute to the program and what they would benefit from receiving.

Each community was grappling with particular challenges, but all were meeting them by building community, lifting up place-based knowledge and going no bigger than human-scale solutions. Superstorms have been battering San Juan and La Marais, Puerto Rico, in quick succession, leaving impossibly narrowing windows for recovery and rebuilding in between. Each left hundreds of thousands of people without fresh food, clean water, electricity, or shelter for months. Export crops like coffee and bananas are stripped from hillsides, stunting important sources of food and income. The trauma of each experience makes anticipation of the next so much worse. In the era of climate emergency, it is hard to know what it would mean to be ready, but agroecology and agroforestry sure seemed more resilience-building than monocultures and commodities markets.

Meanwhile, in Umarkhed, India, intense heat from rising temperatures is made less bearable by recurring drought. The land is parched. Monsoon seasons are no longer reliable water bearers. When prayed-for rains do come, they ferociously wash the land of its poor topsoil – degraded by years of tillage, monocropping, and heavy synthetic inputs. The poor conditions and miniscule yields have resulted in an alarming rise in farmer suicides. In an effort to address all this, the Maati-Paani-Asha Center at Gopikabai Sitaram Gawande College is just beginning modeling and supporting a transition to agroecological farming practices, increase food access and provisioning, improve food marketing, coordinate community water infrastructure improvements, and disseminate novel psychosocial supports. Each of the three elements in the Center's name, which translates to Soil-Water-Hope, are equally vital in the face of climate crisis and despair.

Climate chaos was a more apt descriptor for the scene in Denver, Colorado. Frontline Farming (which you were introduced to a few pages back) is experiencing wild swings in temperature from one day to the next. Later spring snows and earlier fall frosts have begun truncating an already short growing season. And raging wildfires frequently fill the air with choking smoke, dust plants with ash, and turn the sun an angry shade of red.

Even in Bhutan, the land of happiness, all was not entirely well. Though famously carbon-neutral, climate-induced hazards like landslides, mudslides, and flash floods during monsoon season imperil landworkers on the steep slopes and flood-prone riverbeds of the mountain kingdom. Rising unemployment has been prompting youth to leave the land. Plus, pandemic policies that limited imports and pinched supply chains led to shortages of fresh vegetables and other foods. The time for promoting practical and more climate-secure farming approaches that could contribute to food and sustainable livelihoods for Bhutanese youth has come.

Over several months of conversations and convenings, we explored each other's challenges – and more importantly, we started to get inspired by the responses each was mobilizing. As we got to know each other, the contours of a curriculum that covers ecological, agricultural, food systems, and change-shaping knowledge and practices took its first form.

The offer was simple: EcoGather staff would provide the structure and "school skills" to organize the wisdom, perspectives, and insights of partner communities into online educational modules and then freely share the resulting resources among partner communities so that they could learn from each other. The courses would be built in ways that were modular and adaptable. And we would allow all partners ample opportunity to offer input during the development process (or to opt out if a particular course was not clearly relevant to their work).

The EcoGather team also started pushing the boundaries of online education – a learning modality that exists in the ether. We wanted EcoGather to honor the local and lived as the real site of learning. So, we favored the kinds of lessons that come from lived experience, connection to place, and ecological awareness. We also designed exercises and application activities that encourage learners to step away from their devices, into wild nature, out onto their farms, and into their communities to apply and refine what they've learned.

Cognizant of extractivist, imperialist, and supremacist tendencies in both higher education and agricultural research and development, the EcoGather team was especially intentional about how it would convene partners, center their contributions and needs, hold their stories, and share value. To help guide this, we developed principles that, in their full form, help us to (1) handle knowledge and stories with care; (2) attend to the essence of a person, being, community, or place at the core of a narrative; and (3) collect and use stories consensually. The preamble to the "EcoGather Story Ethics" reads:

We seek wisdom from experiences, elders, and ancestors.

We make sense of our experiences in the retelling.

We learn from each other by listening openly.

Meaning making, then, is born of both experience and expression, which can be either solitary or shared.

Choosing to invite others into our experiences and reflections is an act of vulnerability.

Safely releasing our defenses and opening to possibility can only happen when there is trust.

To foster trust, support co-creation, and respectful exchange of knowledges, EcoGather commits to a set of storytelling ethics that center intentionality and ongoing consent.

The very first EcoGather endeavor, a collaboration with Shaun Chamberlin, resulted in a course called *Surviving the Future: A Path Through Tumultuous Times,* the description of which is something of a frame education in an era of collapse:

These are trying times for humanity: it is hard to avoid awareness that things are already bad and rapidly getting worse. And yet, this time is our lifetime – the only time we have to make sense of things and carve the stories of our lives. Perhaps we have a hazy understanding of what's gone wrong, of why so many lives feel hollow, so many futures seem hopeless. Perhaps we recognize that economic systems and social structures are collapsing around us, under the weight of their own deep flaws. But we're less sure of how we might prepare ourselves to weather this period of great transition, or how we might change direction to collectively survive – and even thrive – in the future.

The *Surviving the Future* course – which offers a deep explanation of what is unfolding on our planet, new perspectives on how we might respond, and connection with an accessible and richly fortifying global network of people navigating these times of profound change, together – is a paradigm-shifting experience. Once shifted, learners are eager for courses that are directly relevant to building relationships as part of the natural world and agrelational food systems – and to prepare for collapse. EcoGather's catalog includes courses in Ecology Essentials, Agroecology, Food Systems Thinking, Geographies of Exclusion & Resistance, and a host of skills that land-tenders and good kin will need.

Additionally, in dialog with partners, we found a shared need for education in how to build caring communities, develop empathy, shape and navigate change. We realized that EcoGather could also help activists in environmental justice and food movements to learn from history, from each other, and from a multitude of voices enabling them to become something more than "leaders". Leadership training is everywhere but sharing the living heart of activism across time and place is a very different undertaking. But when people show up to the movements for food systems change they don't always know they are part of and can draw upon a long and very deep history of change shaping.

The best way we had seen change education described was in the work of Octavia E. Butler. So we named our certificate program to honor her notion that change can be shaped by humans but not made. She wrote: "All that you touch, You Change. All that you Change, Changes you. The only lasting truth Is Change."[199] Michelle came to work on the program, acting as the consulting scholar for the *Change Shaping: Connection-based Training for Good Trouble Makers* certificate program and it became another opportunity for building relationships and connections. We brought in change makers from all over the world who work in dozens of kinds of movements to create a web of support and shared wisdom.

EcoGather's *Change Shaping* program starts with the self as the most intimate and smallest unit of change. We need to show up for ourselves and learn the skills necessary to be with trouble. We need a trauma informed stance in the world of change so that we can keep showing up over time – this is how we stay whole as we stay with the trouble. After we have developed the internal skills we can turn outward and build communities where the value of care is the gravitational center. Shared care is a powerful force for both connection and change. Then we dive into activist history and strategy, which helps change shapers to understand the frameworks in which they live and work for a more relational system. Empathy is at the heart of any coalition building between people, groups, communities, and even across the digital world. Empathy is a way to show up, keep showing up, and understand the needs of others so we can show up for their communities too. Finally, we shape change through a story-based framework and build skills for narrative transformation.

EcoGather is emergent. Its first classes were released recently and more are in active stages of co-creation. While it is too soon to proclaim this experiment in relational online education as a transformative force, it is not too early to appreciate how it meets the moment. EcoGather began in March of 2020, just as COVID-19 required separation as an act of care. Its form and substance were influenced by the exigencies and insights of the early 2020s, making it unique as an ecologically and community-centered, collapse aware and responsive type of education. When asked to describe EcoGather, its creative director, Heidi Myers, said, "EcoGather is education that makes sense in a world that does not." Perhaps because it was created not by experts, but through relationships.

Chapter 6

Murmurations

On an especially dreary and bitter day last March, Nicole sat on the concrete floor of her basement surrounded by toilet paper tubes, bags of soil, and seeds that a friend's daughter saved and generously shared. Each time she filled a makeshift cardboard pot and tucked a seed into the soft soil, she whispered: *Seeds hold the past and the future. So do beating human hearts. And stars.* Warmed a little and sometimes happily distracted by the giddy excitement that her husband and sons brought to the task, Nicole was able to sit on the cold floor for longer than should have been tolerable, creating the conditions for creation. After hours of seeding and speaking this mantra, Nicole felt two truths deeply: (1) everything is connected across time, space, and form, and (2) food is a way into and around that web of connection.

Food systems have the potential to re-form as dense, supple and sustaining webs of connections – social connections among humans, eco-spiritual connections between humans and more-than-human kin. These connections will, first and foremost, reassemble within place-based communities at scales that are readily discernible. But they will also sometimes stretch across the globe, among those who merit trust. Plant, animal, fungi, and mineral material – the stuff of food – will be able to move through these webs and their remnants returned for re-substantiation.

This relational approach is not a quick fix for anything – it is the work of generations. We may not, as one of Michelle's favorite sayings goes, finish the work, but we are obligated to start it. As you set out or stride further into your relational journey, we leave you with a few ideas to carry in your pocket. Grab hold of them when you need some comfort or encouragement. We know we haven't offered you a plan or prescription. We think, though, that we've offered you some things that are more irresistible – an invitation to relationship with new ideas and kin, an entirely new way of being. So use this book as a touchstone, an idea generator, a way to open conversations, and a way to feed your soul.

The poet Alexis Pauline Gumbs is a sweet companion and her books may help soothe your spirit. After noting that any ecological or relational approach is necessarily for the long term, she reminds us that "[t]he intentional practice of growing a vision for a lovingly transformational way of life in an economic system that seeks to make our lives and love unthinkable feels ambitious and risky. It is actually as simple as remembering who we are, what life is, and acting accordingly, for the rest of our lives... and with an intergenerationally accountable relationship to the future with us always."[200]

Make moves toward relationship, away from transactional arrangements, especially extractive ones. But don't obsess over every bite of food you put into your mouth. Binary thinking and perfectionist tendencies reduce the complexity of our contexts and the nuances of all our relationships. This kind of thinking can also drive us mad either by convincing us that the options available are never good enough and making us feel perpetually inadequate. Let's see this in action: Is buying fruit from a local orchardist who sometimes sprays his heirloom apple, pear, and cherry trees with synthetic fungicides to avoid the loss of many trees relational or transactional? Is that question even worth asking? Is it more or less relational than buying apples from a biodynamic orchard across the country? What about the wax and pesticide coated Red Delicious from Walmart that the elderly widow across the street offers your child: is it relational to accept or reject her gift? There is never just one right answer. Binary mental models and norms are themselves anti-relational

– so ditch them. Instead, do the work to figure out what kinds of relationships you most want to have with the Earth, with other people, and with more-than-human kin through food and move toward them.

Transactional & Extractive Orientation	Relational & Empathic Orientation
Takes whatever it can get without damaging reputation	Gives whatever it can offer without imperiling itself
Gives only when it can take something specific in return	Gives (or gifts) without expecting something specific in return
Quantifies & focuses on how much	Qualifies & focuses on impacts
Focuses on the short to mid-term gains and losses	Balances needs across time
Limits long-term thinking to less than one lifetime	Extends long-term thinking across generations
Keeps receipts and tallies	Offers gratitude and trust
Primarily motivated by self- and corporate-Interest	Typically motivated by mutual thriving and planetary well-being
Demands attention be stretched and splintered	Purposefully directs and opens attention
Judges and accepts or rejects firmly	Remains receptive
Broader interests limited to living humans or use value of nature	Broader interests include past and future humans, intrinsic value of nature
Careful and Calculating	Care-full and Cultivating
Adds up enjoyments	Experiences enchantment
Draws tight circles of care, encompassing self, family, and affinity groups	Widens circles of care across difference, location, time, and species

Transactional conditioning is something that most of us have to unlearn. Plus, it can be really challenging to change how we show up and respond when we're facing an unstable present and an uncertain future. In moments of high stress and anxiety – moments when it is most important to stay connected – it is all too easy to revert to self-interested and transactional behaviors. We're so familiar with transactional terrain that we often feel lost in the woods when we try to move towards the relational. To help with wayfinding, we've mapped some characteristics on each end of the spectrum.

Moving toward relationality will take our energy and attention – but with each move we make, these won't seem as scarce. In his effort to make degrowth seem irresistible, Jason Hickel observes, "When people live in a fair, caring society, where everyone has equal access to social goods, they don't have to spend their time worrying about how to cover their basic needs day to day – they can enjoy the art of living. And instead of feeling they are in constant competition with their neighbours, they can build bonds of social solidarity."[201] There's a bit of a chicken and egg conundrum here – we need time to make society fairer and more caring and we get time once it is. But, if we can help each other carve some space to take the first steps, the trail opens up and time loses its fraying edges.

Have humility as you go. We cannot stress enough that pride, acquisitiveness, and self-seeking goals helped create this system we need to break down and compost. Our intellectual, emotional, and even spiritual humility is necessary to make relational shifts. This may be the hardest part of the entire change process. Humility comes hard to humans. But, when forced through circumstance to confront our mess and the ways in which we have been responsible for creating and maintaining it, we are driven to the humility we need to reassess our past and reenvision our future, our relationships, and our place in all of it.

Pay attention to who is on this journey, looking for unlikely kin who are moving with you as this emergent way of being unfolds. Build bridges with anyone and everyone you can –

human and beyond. Expect it to be hard sometimes. Bridge building takes courage and strength. Confronting power on its own turf is hard – and most of the world belongs to the agricapitalist system at the moment. We should approach it with awareness that john powell summed well in a speech: "I have a word of caution for you from my good friend, bell hooks. She says, 'Bridges are made to walk on. So when you first become a bridge between two communities that see themselves in opposition, you will be walked on and occasionally, hopefully not too often, you will be stomped on.' But I say this, 'If the world is not bridged, if we do not have more bridges in the world, if we continue to break, we won't have a world.'" So, your work as bridgers, even though sometimes you'll be walked on, occasionally stomped on, is critical for our survival.[202]

That's actually okay. Ross Gay, our champion of delight, tells us that joy is inextricably connected to both loss and labor – internal excavations, physical exertion, relational exchanges, and deep carework. We must open our bridging selves to the pain and stay with the trouble of grief and loss to get to the joys that wait beyond. Ross has a hunch "that joy is an ember for or precursor to wild and unpredictable and transgressive and unboundaried solidarity. And that that solidarity might incite further joy. Which might incite further solidarity. And on and on… [J]oy, emerging from our common sorrow… might depolarize us and de-atomize us enough that we can consider what, in common, we love."[203]

We are not yet at the place where we are having wild-yet-serious public and political conversations about common love. But also the signals for love, care, relationship, and connection are getting louder and harder to ignore. When you want to retreat, which is a reasonable response to overwhelm, remember that there are so many others who wish to respond to our current and coming crises with kindness, connection and courage. Douglas Brooks, Sanskritist and occasional opiner on all things community, reminds us that we are the company we keep – so keep good company. And do so with the knowledge that you can't succeed alone. We have a place in this world that is ours, it is small, but we can be powerful when we work together for good. You are in the company of the tallest peaks and the most verdant valleys, with elders and wise people from places you may never have heard of, you keep company with the mushrooms, the aspen trees, the sheep and the salmon, and with a growing number of people who feel and see the world as you do. You are an essential part of the community of the future and you are not alone.

The only way to survive is by taking care of one another.
—Grace Lee Boggs

Notes

Chapter One

1. Donella Meadows, *Thinking in Systems* (White River Junction, VT: Chelsea Green, 2008).
2. Ibid.
3. Donella Meadows, "Dancing With Systems," *The Academy for Systems Change* (blog), accessed October 28, 2022, https://donellameadows.org/archives/dancing-with-systems/.
4. "Angel Kyodo Williams – The World Is Our Field of Practice," The On Being Project, accessed October 25, 2022, https://onbeing.org/programs/angel-kyodo-williams-the-world-is-our-field-of-practice/.
5. "john a. powell | Othering & Belonging Institute," accessed October 26, 2022, https://belonging.berkeley.edu/john-powell.
6. Donna Haraway, *Staying with the Trouble: Making Kin in the Chthulucene* (Durham, NC: Duke University Press, 2016).
7. Sapiens, "Would Our Early Ancestors Have Watched the Super Bowl?," SAPIENS, January 31, 2019, https://www.sapiens.org/archaeology/history-of-fire-super-bowl/.
8. Auerbach, Michelle. "Storytelling as a Trauma Sensitive Technology for Change in Individuals, Organizations, and Communities." PhD thesis, Graduate Theological Foundation, 2021.
9. Roseann Liu and Savannah Shange, "Toward Thick Solidarity: Theorizing Empathy in Social Justice Movements," *Radical History Review* 2018, no. 131 (May 1, 2018): 189–98, https://doi.org/10.1215/01636545-4355341.
10. Patty Krawec, *Becoming Kin* (Pin Blush, NY: Broadleaf Books, 2022).

11. Clore G.L., Huntsinger J.R. (2007). How emotions inform judgment and regulate thought. Trends in Cognitive Sciences, 11(9), 393–9.

12. Vilayanur S. Ramachandran and Diane Rogers-Ramachandran, "Mind the Gap," Scientific American, accessed October 26, 2022, https://doi.org/10.1038/scientificamericanmind0405-100.

13. "A Growing Culture | WE BELIEVE IN FOOD SOVEREIGNTY. FOR EVERYONE. EVERYWHERE.," accessed November 14, 2022, https://www.agrowingculture.org/.

14. Shaun Chamberlin, "Humanity - Not Just a Virus with Shoes," Dark Optimism (blog), August 6, 2019, https://www.darkoptimism.org/2019/08/06/humanity-not-just-a-virus-with-shoes/.

15. "Bridging and Breaking | Othering & Belonging Institute," accessed October 28, 2022, https://belonging.berkeley.edu/bridging-and-breaking.

16. From an interview with Selassie Atadika April 11, 2020 and partially published in Michelle Auerbach, Resilience: The Life Saving Skill of Story (Washington D.C.: Changemakers Books, 2020).

17. Robin Wall Kimmerer, Braiding Sweetgrass, Footsteps of Nanabozho (10–15 pages in).

18. Williams-Forson, Psyche (2014). "'I Haven't Eaten If I Don't Have My Soup and Fufu': Cultural Preservation through Food and Foodways among Ghanaian Migrants in the United States". Africa Today. 61 (1): 69–87. doi:10.2979/africatoday.61.1.69

Gilroy, Paul (1997). Diaspora and the Detours of Identity. Open University Press.

Chapter Two

19. Donella Meadows, *Thinking in Systems* (White River Junction, VT: Chelsea Green, 2008).

20. Caitlyn Hutson, "From Bean to Cup: How the Coffee Supply Chain Work – Atlas Coffee Club," *Atlas Coffee Club Blog | Club Culture* (blog), September 9, 2017, https://club.atlascoffeeclub.com/coffee-supply-chain/.

21. Sushma Naithani, "The Origins of Agriculture," June 8, 2021, https://open.oregonstate.education/cultivatedplants/chapter/agriculture/.

22. Leah Bayens, Cultivating Ecological Agrarianism: Sustainable Agriculture in American Literature: A dissertation submitted in partial fulfillment of the requirements for the degree of Doctor of Philosophy in the College of Arts and Sciences at the University of Kentucky (Lexington, KY, 2012).

23. Dan Allosso, "Green Revolution," accessed November 14, 2022, https://mlpp.pressbooks.pub/americanenvironmentalhistory/chapter/chapter-8-green-revolution/.

24. March 15 and 2016 Danielle Sedbrook, "2,4-D: The Most Dangerous Pesticide You've Never Heard Of," NRDC, accessed November 14, 2022, https://www.nrdc.org/stories/24-d-most-dangerous-pesticide-youve-never-heard.

25. OCSPP US EPA, "2,4-D," Overviews and Factsheets, September 22, 2014, https://www.epa.gov/ingredients-used-pesticide-products/24-d.

26. Michal Mazur, "Six Ways Drones Are Revolutionizing Agriculture," MIT Technology Review, accessed November 14, 2022, https://www.technologyreview.com/2016/07/20/158748/six-ways-drones-are-revolutionizing-agriculture/.

27. How Agriculture Becomes Agribusiness, (September 7, 2018) archived at https://web.archive.org/web/20201130195442/ http://agritechtalk.com/2018/09/07/how-agriculture-becomes-agribusiness/.

28. Wes Jackson, Nature as Measure (Counterpoint, 2011).

29. PBES (2019): Global assessment report on biodiversity and ecosystem services of the Intergovernmental Science-Policy Platform on Biodiversity and Ecosystem Services. E. S. Brondizio, J. Settele, S. Díaz, and H. T. Ngo (editors). IPBES secretariat, Bonn, Germany. 1148 pages. https://doi.org/10.5281/zenodo.3831673

30. EC Ellis, K Klein Goldewijk, S Siebert, D Lightman, N Ramankutty, Anthropogenic transformation of the biomes, 1700 to 2000. *Glob Ecol Biogeogr* 19, 589–606 (2010).

31. "Agriculture - Water, Environmental, United States, History, Impact, EPA, Soil, Pesticide, Chemicals, Industrial, Toxic, World, Human, Power, Use, Health, Traditional Agricultural Systems," accessed December 12, 2022, http://www.pollutionissues.com/A-Bo/Agriculture.html.

32. "Sustainability Pathways: Sustainability and Organic Livestock," accessed November 14, 2022, https://www.fao.org/nr/sustainability/sustainability-and-livestock.

33. Ibid.

34. Rulli et al., "The water-land-food nexus of first-generation biofuels." Sci Rep 6, 22521 (2016). https://doi.org/10.1038/srep22521

35. "Cutting down Forests: What Are the Drivers of Deforestation?," Our World in Data, accessed November 14, 2022, https://ourworldindata.org/what-are-drivers-deforestation.

36. Scheer, Roddy and Doug Moss, "Deforestation and Its Extreme Effect on Global Warming." Scientific American, (November 2012).

37. De Sy et al., "Land use patterns and related carbon losses following deforestation in South America." Environmental Research Letters, 10, no.122015 (November 2015)https://doi.org/10.1088/1748-9326/10/12/124004

38. Gibbs et al., "Tropical forests were the primary sources of new agricultural land in the 1980s and 1990s." PNAS 107, no. 38 (August 2010). https://doi.org/10.1073/pnas.0910275107.

39. David Pimentel and Michael Burgess, "Soil Erosion Threatens Food Production," Agriculture 3, no. 3 (September 2013): 443–63, https://doi.org/10.3390/agriculture3030443.

40. David Pimentel, "Soil Erosion: A Food and Environmental Threat," Environment, Development and Sustainability 8, no. 1 (February 1, 2006): 119–37, https://doi.org/10.1007/s10668-005-1262-8.

41. Ibid.

42. "How Much of the World's Food Production Is Dependent on Pollinators?," Our World in Data, accessed November 14, 2022, https://ourworldindata.org/pollinator-dependence.

43. Lorenzo Rosa et al., "Global Agricultural Economic Water Scarcity," Science Advances 6, no. 18 (April 29, 2020): eaaz6031, https://doi.org/10.1126/sciadv.aaz6031.

44. "Groundwater Use in the United States | U.S. Geological Survey," accessed December 12, 2022, https://www.usgs.gov/special-topics/water-science-school/science/groundwater-use-united-states?qt-science_center_objects=0#qt-science_center_objects.

45. (Konikow & Kennedy, 2005).

46. July 21 and 2022 Courtney Lindwall, "Industrial Agricultural Pollution 101," NRDC, accessed December 12, 2022, https://www.nrdc.org/stories/industrial-agricultural-pollution-101.

47. "Global Assessment Report on Biodiversity and Ecosystem Services," IPBES secretariat, May 17, 2019, https://ipbes.net/node/35274.

48. Sean L. Maxwell et al., "Biodiversity: The Ravages of Guns, Nets and Bulldozers," *Nature* 536, no. 7615 (August 2016): 143–45, https://doi.org/10.1038/536143a.

49. "FAO – News Article: Pollinators Vital to Our Food Supply under Threat," accessed November 14, 2022, https://www.fao.org/news/story/en/item/384726/icode/.

50. Willige, Andrea, "75% of crops depend on pollinators - they must be protected." World Economic Forum (December 2019). https://www.weforum.org/agenda/2019/12/protect-pollinators-food-security-biodiversity-agriculture/.

51. "Seeking New Agreements – Agricultural Biodiversity," Agroecology Now!, November 24, 2020, https://www.agroecologynow.com/seeking-new-ways-to-work-with-nature-enhancing-agricultural-biodiversity/.

52. "Mainstreaming agrobiodiversity in sustainable food systems: Scientific foundations for an agrobiodiversity index." Bioversity International, https://cgspace.cgiar.org/handle/10568/www.bioversityinternational.org/mainstreaming-agrobiodiversity/. (2017). https://cgspace.cgiar.org/handle/10568/www.bioversityinternational.org/mainstreaming-agrobiodiversity/.

53. Pat Mooney, "Blocking the Chain: Industrial Food Chain Concentration, Big Data Platforms and Food Sovereignty Solutions" (ETC Group, 2018).

54. "Biodiversity and the Livestock Sector: Guidelines for Quantitative Assessment" (Rome, Italy: Livestock Environmental Assessment and Performance (LEAP) Partnership, 2019).

55. Esri's StoryMaps team, "(Farm) Animal Planet," ArcGIS StoryMaps, June 16, 2022, https://storymaps.arcgis.com/stories/58ae71f58fd7418294f34c4f841895d8.

56. Vandana Shiva, "Monocultures of the Mind: Perspectives on Biodiversity and Biotechnology" (Zed Books, 1993)

57. For a modern example of this loss please read Frank Swain, "The Banana as We Know It Is Going Extinct. Could Gene Editing Save It?," Massive Science, July 23, 2020, https://massivesci.com/articles/cavendish-bananas-extinction-rebirth/.

58. Damian Carrington, "Humans Just 0.01% of All Life but Have Destroyed 83% of Wild Mammals – Study," *The Guardian*, May 21, 2018, sec. Environment, https://www.theguardian.com/environment/2018/may/21/human-race-just-001-of-all-life-but-has-destroyed-over-80-of-wild-mammals-study

59. Mood, Alison. 2010. Review of How Many Fish Are Caught Each Year? In Worse Things Happen at Sea: The Welfare of Wild Caught Fish, 70–71. Fishcount.org. http://www.fishcount.org.uk/published/std/fishcountchapter19.pdf

60. Bar-On, Yinon M., Rob Phillips, and Ron Milo. "The Biomass Distribution on Earth." Proceedings of the National Academy of Sciences 115, no. 25 (2018): 6506–11. https://doi.org/10.1073/pnas.1711842115.

61. Britten, Gregory, Carlos Duarte, and Boris Worm. "Recovery of Assessed Global Fish Stocks Remains Uncertain." Proceedings of the National Academy of Sciences 118, no. 31 (2021). https://doi.org/10.1073/pnas.2108532118.

62. Garcia, Serge M., and Andrew A. Rosenberg. "Food Security and Marine Capture Fisheries: Characteristics, Trends, Drivers and Future Perspectives." Philosophical Transactions of the Royal Society B: Biological Sciences 365, no. 1554 (2010): 2869–80. https://doi.org/10.1098/rstb.2010.0171.

63. U. N. Environment, "UNEP Food Waste Index Report 2021," UNEP – UN Environment Programme, March 4, 2021, http://www.unep.org/resources/report/unep-food-waste-index-report-2021.

64. "ReFED – Food Waste Monitor," accessed December 12, 2022, https://insights-engine.refed.org/food-waste-monitor?break_by=destination&indicator=tons-waste&sec tor=residential&view=detail&year=2019.

65. M. Crippa et al., "Food Systems Are Responsible for a Third of Global Anthropogenic GHG Emissions," *Nature Food* 2, no. 3 (March 2021): 198–209, https://doi.org/10.1038/s43016-021-00225-9.

66. Michael Clark, "We Need to Talk about Food When We Talk about Climate," University of Oxford Future of Food, accessed October 28, 2022, https://www.leap.ox.ac.uk/article/we-need-to-talk-about-food-when-we-talk-about-climate

67. Hannah Ritchie, Max Roser, and Pablo Rosado, "CO_2 and Greenhouse Gas Emissions," *Our World in Data*, May 11, 2020, https://ourworldindata.org/emissions-by-sector.

"Food Production Is Responsible for One-Quarter of the World's Greenhouse Gas Emissions," Our World in Data, accessed December 12, 2022, https://ourworldindata.org/food-ghg-emissions.

68. Johan Rockström et al., "A Safe Operating Space for Humanity," *Nature* 461, no. 7263 (September 2009): 472–75, https://doi.org/10.1038/461472a.

Marco Springmann et al., "Options for Keeping the Food System within Environmental Limits," *Nature* 562, no. 7728 (October 2018): 519–25, https://doi.org/10.1038/s41586-018-0594-0.

69. Johan Rockström et al., "Planetary Boundaries: Exploring the Safe Operating Space for Humanity," *Ecology and Society* 14, no. 2 (November 18, 2009), https://doi.org/10.5751/ES-03180-140232.

70. Johan Rockström et al., "A Safe Operating Space for Humanity," *Nature* 461, no. 7263 (September 2009): 472–75, https://doi.org/10.1038/461472a.

71. "Protecting Planetary Boundaries: Aligning the SDGs to Ensure Humankind's Future," *SDG Action* (blog), June 16, 2021, https://sdg-action.org/protecting-planetary-boundaries-aligning-the-sdgs-to-ensure-humankinds-future/.

72. Bon Appétit Management Company Foundation (BAMCO) and United Farm Workers (UFW). Inventory of Farmworker Issues and Protections in the United States. (March 2011)., available at http://www.ufw.org/pdf/farmworkerinventory_0401_2011.pdf; Food Chain Workers Alliance (FCWA). The Hands That Feed Us: Challenges and opportunities for workers along the food chain. (2012). Available at http://foodchainworkers.org/wp-content/uploads/2012/06/Hands-That-Feed-Us-Report.pdf

73. "Global Estimates of Modern Slavery" (International Labour Organization and Walk Free Foundation, 2017). https://www.ilo.org/wcmsp5/groups/public/---dgreports/---dcomm/documents/publication/wcms_575479.pdf

74. The Key to Saving the Restaurant Industry Post COVID-19" (One Fair Wage, n.d.), https://onefairwage.site/wp-content/uploads/2022/05/OFW_FactSheet_USA.pdf.

75. Holt-Giménez, E., Shattuck, A., Altieri, M., Herren, H., Gliessman, S. (2012). We already grow.

76. Ibid.

77. Paul West et al., "Leverage Points for Improving Global Food Security and the Environment," *Science* 345, no. 6194 (July 2014).

78. FAO, IFAD, UNICEF, WFP and WHO. 2020. The State of Food Security and Nutrition in the World 2020. Transforming food systems for affordable healthy diets. Rome, FAO.

79. 1,000 Days. (2021, January 4). 1,000 Days. https://thousanddays.org/

80. Food Security Information Network (FSIN). 2020. 2020 Global report on food crises: Joint analysis for better

decisions. Rome, Italy and Washington, DC: Food and Agriculture Organization (FAO); World Food Programme (WFP); and International Food Policy Research Institute (IFPRI). https://www.fsinplatform.org/global-report-food-crises-2020

81. "The Role of Diets in Shaping the Global Burden of Disease – Global Panel," November 25, 2015, https://www.glopan.org/news/the-role-of-diets-in-shaping-the-global-burden-of-disease/.

   "Protecting Planetary Boundaries: Aligning the SDGs to Ensure Humankind's Future," *SDG Action* (blog), June 16, 2021, https://sdg-action.org/protecting-planetary-boundaries-aligning-the-sdgs-to-ensure-humankinds-future/.

82. Damian Carrington, "True Cost of Cheap Food Is Health and Climate Crises, Says Commission," *The Guardian*, July 16, 2019, sec. Environment, https://www.theguardian.com/environment/2019/jul/16/true-cost-of-cheap-food-is-health-and-climate-crises-says-commission.

83. Ibid.

84. Alexandratos, N. and Bruinsma, J. (2012) World Agriculture towards 2030/2050: The 2012 Revision. ESA Working Paper No. 12-03, FAO, Rome.

85. Jonathan Russell Latham, "The Myth of a Food Crisis," in *Rethinking Food and Agriculture* (Elsevier, 2020), 93–111.

86. Jonathan Latham, "Agriculture's Greatest Myth," Independent Science News | Food, Health and Agriculture Bioscience News, April 12, 2021, https://www.independentsciencenews.org/commentaries/agricultures-greatest-myth/.

87. "War in Ukraine Drives Global Food Crisis" (Rome, Italy: World Food Programme, 2022). https://docs.wfp.org/api/documents/WFP-0000140700/download/?_ga=2.261400653.112665972.1667822338-1348529574.1667822338

88. Adinor José Capellesso et al., "Economic and Environmental Impacts of Production Intensification in Agriculture: Comparing Transgenic, Conventional, and Agroecological Maize Crops," *Agroecology and Sustainable Food Systems*, January 26, 2016, https://www.tandfonline.com/doi/full/10.1080/21683565.2015.1128508.

89. "With Climate Chaos, Who Will Feed Us? The Industrial Food Chain or the Peasant Food Web" (Action Group on Erosion, Technology, and Concentration, 2014). https://www.etcgroup.org/sites/www.etcgroup.org/files/web_who_will_feed_us_with_notes_0.pdf

90. "Smallholders Produce One-Third of the World's Food, Less than Half of What Many Headlines Claim," Our World in Data, accessed December 12, 2022, https://ourworldindata.org/smallholder-food-production.

91. Chris Smaje. 2020. *A Small Farm Future: Making the Case for a Society Built Around Local Economies, Self-Provisioning, Agricultural Diversity and a Shared Earth.* Chelsea Green.

Chapter Three

92. Jason Hickel, Twitter https://twitter.com/jasonhickel/status/1515977488110915587

93. Susan George, "A Short History of Neoliberalism," Transnational Institute, March 24, 1999, https://www.tni.org/en/article/short-history-neoliberalism.

94. Ibid.

95. George Monbiot, "Neoliberalism – the Ideology at the Root of All Our Problems," *The Guardian*, April 15, 2016, sec. Books, https://www.theguardian.com/books/2016/apr/15/neoliberalism-ideology-problem-george-monbiot. Also *Naomi Klein on Global Neoliberalism | Big Think*, 2012.

96. Naomi Klein, *This Changes Everything: Capitalism vs. The Climate* (New York, NY: Simon & Schuster Paperbacks, 2015).

97. Mariana Mazzucato, *Mission Economy: A Moonshot Guide to Changing Capitalism* (New York, NY: Harper Business, 2021).

98. IPES, Too Big to Feed, https://www.ipes-food.org/_img/ upload/files/Concentration_FullReport.pdf 2018; https:// www.theguardian.com/commentisfree/2021/apr/05/bill-gates-climate-crisis-farmland and https://landreport. com/2022/08/farmer-bill/; https://www.theguardian.com/ environment/ng-interactive/2021/jul/14/food-monopoly-meals-profits-data-investigation

99. EWG's Farm Subsidy Database, "EWG's Farm Subsidy Database," accessed December 12, 2022, http://farm.ewg. org/region.php. https://farm.ewg.org/region.php#:~:text= 69%20percent%20of%20farms%20in,subsidy%20 payments%20%2D%20according%20to%20USDA

100. EWG's Farm Subsidy Database, "EWG's Farm Subsidy Database," accessed December 12, 2022, http://farm.ewg. org/progdetail.php?fips=00000&progcode=tot alfarm&page=conc&regionname=theUnitedSt ates&_ga=2.177003565.921975141.1670563341-971440656.1668098697.

101. EWG, "Interactive Map: Farm Subsidies Ballooned Under Trump," accessed November 14, 2022, http://www.ewg. org/interactive-maps/2021-farm-subsidies-ballooned-under-trump/; EWG, "The United States Farm Subsidy Information" accessed November 14, 2022, https:// farm.ewg.org/region.php#:~:text=69%20percent%20 of%20farms%20in,subsidy%20payments%20%2D%20 according%20to%20USDA.

102. EWG's Farm Subsidy Database, "EWG's Farm Subsidy Database," accessed November 14, 2022, http://farm.ewg. org/region.php?fips=00000&regionname=theUnitedStates.

103. Dan Charles, "Farmers Got Billions From Taxpayers In 2019, And Hardly Anyone Objected," *NPR*, December 31, 2019,

https://www.npr.org/sections/thesalt/2019/12/31/790261705/farmers-got-billions-from-taxpayers-in-2019-and-hardly-anyone-objected.

104. "USDA Gave Almost 100 Percent of Trump's Trade War Bailout to White Farmers," The Counter, July 29, 2019, https://thecounter.org/usda-trump-trade-war-bailout-white-farmers-race/.

105. "Revealed: the true extent of America's food monopolies, and who pays the price," The Guardian, July 14, 2021, https://www.theguardian.com/environment/ng-interactive/2021/jul/14/food-monopoly-meals-profits-data-investigation

106. Phillip McMichael, "Historicizing Food Sovereignty: A Food Regime Perspective," Docslib, September 2013, https://docslib.org/doc/9655723/historicizing-food-sovereignty-a-food-regime-perspective.

107. Charles Z. Levkoe and N. Saul, "The Community Food Centre: Building Community, a Healthy Environment and Social Justice Through Food," in *Recipes for Success: A Celebration of Food Security Work in Canada* (Chicago, IL: Independent Publishers Group, 2005).

108. Patel and Moore, A History of the World in Seven Cheap Things: A Guide to Capitalism, Nature, and the Future of the Planet.

109. Robin James, "Notes On A Theory Of Multi-Racial White Supremacist Patriarchy, Aka MRWaSP," accessed June 30, 2019, https://www.its-her-factory.com/2013/11/notes-on-a-theory-of-multi-racial-white-supremacist-patriarchy-aka-mrwasp/.

110. Elizabeth Schussler Fiorenza, *Wisdom Ways: Introducing Feminist Biblical Interpretation* (Maryknoll, NY: Orbis Books, 2001).

111. Patty Krawec, "To Be Good Kin," *Midnight Sun* (blog), February 14, 2022, https://www.midnightsunmag.ca/to-be-good-kin/.

112. Heather McGhee, *The Sum of Us: What Racism Costs Everyone and How We Can Prosper Together* (One World, 2021).

113. See Arlie Hochschild and Anne Machung, *Second Shift* (New York: Penguin Books, 2012). Also "How Gender Equality Can Transform Food Systems and Protect Us From Climate Change Disasters," *CGIAR* (blog), accessed October 27, 2022, https://www.cgiar.org/news-events/news/how-gender-equality-can-transform-food-systems-and-protect-us-from-climate-change-disasters/.

114. Gus Wezerek and Kristen R. Ghodsee, "Women's Unpaid Labor is Worth $10,900,000,000,000," New York Times, March 5, 2020, https://www.nytimes.com/interactive/2020/03/04/opinion/women-unpaid-labor.html.

115. Olga Khazan, "Food Swamps Are the New Food Deserts," The Atlantic, December 28, 2017, https://www.theatlantic.com/health/archive/2017/12/food-swamps/549275/.

116. "About Me," Karen Washington, accessed October 28, 2022, https://www.karenthefarmer.com/about.

117. Stray Dog Institute, "What Is the Difference Between Food Apartheid and Food Deserts?," *Stray Dog Institute* (blog), May 19, 2022, https://straydoginstitute.org/food-apartheid/.

118. S. Margot Finn, *Discriminating Taste: How Class Anxiety Created the American Food Revolution* (2017)

119. Robin L. Goldberg, "What Is "Healthism?," *Robyn L. Goldberg* (blog), July 30, 2018, https://askaboutfood.com/what-is-healthism-august-2018/.

120. Reesmaa Menakem, *My Grandmother's Hands* (Las Vegas, NV: Central Recovery Press, 2017).

121. Isabel Foxen Duke, "Letting Go of 'Health-Ism' and Related Panic," Isabel Foxen Duke, November 17, 2016, https://isabelfoxenduke.com/letting-go-of-health-ism-and-related-anxiety/.

122. Himanshu Vig and Deshmukh Roshan, "Weight Loss and Weight Management Diet Market by Product Type: Global Opportunity Analysis and Industry Forecast, 2021–2027" (Allied Market Research, 2021) available at https://www.alliedmarketresearch.com/weight-loss-management-diet-market

123. Your Fat Friend, "The Bizarre and Racist History of the BMI," *Elemental* (blog), October 18, 2019, https://elemental.medium.com/the-bizarre-and-racist-history-of-the-bmi-7d8dc2aa33bb. And Christy Harrison, *Anti-Diet: Reclaim Your Time, Money, Well-Being, and Happiness through Intuitive Eating* (New York: Little Brown Spark, 2019)

124. Sarah Evans, "Is Prison Labor the Future of Our Food System?," Food First, accessed October 28, 2022, https://archive.foodfirst.org/is-prison-labor-the-future-of-our-food-system/. Citing "Ag Labor in the PIC Pdf," Google Docs, accessed October 28, 2022, https://drive.google.com/file/u/0/d/1ZWdBH5zlKbV6K6subbGMm4nUMY3_ZZgJ/view?pli=1&usp=embed_facebook.

125. "Global Estimates of Modern Slavery: Forced Labor and Forced Marriage" (International Labour Organization, Walk Free, and International Organization for Migration, 2022) available at https://www.ilo.org/wcmsp5/groups/public/---ed_norm/---ipec/documents/publication/wcms_854733.pdf

126. "To Meet Farm-Labor Shortages, Idaho Puts Inmates on the Job," Successful Farming, October 19, 2017, https://www.agriculture.com/news/to-meet-farm-labor-shortages-idaho-puts-inmates-on-the-job.

127. William Horne, "The Vampire's Bacon," in *Vegan Entanglements: Dismantling Racial and Carceral Capitalism*, ed. Z. Zane McNeill (Brooklyn, NY: Lantern Publishing and Media, 2022).

128. We believe Mariame first said this on Twitter (@ prisonculture) in 2018. The advice struck a chord and was shared everywhere during the summer of 2020. Later this year, we will all be able to learn more about what she meant by reading her forthcoming book with Kelly Hayes: Let This Radicalize You: Organizing and the Revolution of Reciprocal Care, Haymarket Books, 2023.

129. "The Roots of 'Radical,'" accessed January 1, 2023, https://www.merriam-webster.com/words-at-play/radical-word-history.

130. Beronda Montgomery, Lessons From Plants, (Cambridge, MA: Harvard University Press, 2021).

131. Donella Meadows and et al., *Limits to Growth: A Report For the Club of Rome Project on the Predicament of Mankind* (New York, NY: Universe Books, 1972). https://www.library.dartmouth.edu/digital/digital-collections/limits-growth; Christian Parenti, "'The Limits to Growth': A Book That Launched a Movement," December 5, 2012, https://www.thenation.com/article/archive/limits-growth-book-launched-movement/.

132. "Collapse Now and Avoid the Rush," Resilience, June 5, 2012, https://www.resilience.org/stories/2012-06-06/collapse-now-and-avoid-rush/.

133. David Fleming, https://leanlogic.online/glossary/climacteric/, accessed January 1, 2023.

134. David Fleming, https://leanlogic.online/glossary/system-scale-rule/, accessed January 1, 2023.

135. Shaun Chamberlin, https://www.darkoptimism.org/about/

136. "Breaking Down: Collapse," Buzzsprout, accessed October 27, 2022, https://collapsepod.buzzsprout.com/1403161.

137. David E. H. J. Gernaat, Climate change impacts on renewable energy supply. Nature Climate Change, 2021.

138. "The Growing Role of Minerals and Metals for a Low Carbon Future" (Washington D.C.: World Bank Group, 2017).

139. *Why Renewables Can't Save the Planet – Michael Shellenberger*, 2019, https://www.youtube.com/watch?v=N-yALPEpV4w.

140. Hannah Ritchie, Pablo Rosado, and Max Roser, "Meat and Dairy Production," *Our World in Data*, August 25, 2017, https://ourworldindata.org/meat-production.

141. Naomi Klein, *This Changes Everything: Capitalism vs. The Climate* (Simon & Schuster Paperbacks, 2015).

142. Arundhati Roy, "The Pandemic Is a Portal," *Financial Times*, April 3, 2020.

143. *N.K. Jemisin's Master Class in World Building | The Ezra Klein Show*, 2018, https://www.youtube.com/watch?v=I6xyFQhbsjQ.

144. Rachel Kaadzi Ghansah, Samuel R. Delany, The Art of Fiction No. 210, PARIS REV., https://www.theparisreview.org/interviews/6088/samuel-r-delany-the-art-of-fiction-no-210- samuel-r-delany.

145. Imogen Malpas, "Climate Fiction Is a Vital Tool for Producing Better Planetary Futures," *The Lancet Planetary Health* 5, no. 1 (January 1, 2021): e12–13, https://doi.org/10.1016/S2542-5196(20)30307-7.

Chapter Four

146. "Leverage Points: Places to Intervene in a System," *The Academy for Systems Change* (blog), accessed October 26, 2022, https://donellameadows.org/archives/leverage-points-places-to-intervene-in-a-system/.

147. Mary K. Hendrickson et al., "The Food System: Concentration and Its Impacts: A Special Report to the Family Farm Alliance," November 19, 2020. https://farmaction.us//wp-content/uploads/2020/11/Hendrickson-et-al.-2020.-Concentration-and-Its-Impacts-FINAL.pdf.
Claire Kelloway and Sarah Miller, "Food and Power: Addressing Monopolization in America's Food System" (Open Markets Institute, March 2019), https://static1.

squarespace.com/static/5e449c8c3ef68d752f3e70dc/t/ 5ea9fa6c2c1e9c460038ec5b/1588198002769/190322_ MonopolyFoodReport-v7.pdf.

Julie Creswell, "Beef Prices Are Rising as Bottlenecks Limit Supply – The New York Times," accessed November 14, 2022, https://www.nytimes.com/2021/06/23/business/beef-prices.html.

148. Schismenos, Alexandros; Niaros, Vasilis; Lemos, Lucas (2021). "A Genealogy of Cosmolocalism". In Ramos, José; Bauwens, Michel; Ede, Sharon; Wong, James (eds.). *Cosmolocal Reader*. Futures Lab. pp. 37–51. ISBN 978-0-9953546-3-0.

149. https://farmhack.org, accessed January 1, 2023

150. "Farm Hack: A Commons for Agricultural Innovation | Heinrich Böll Stiftung," Heinrich-Böll-Stiftung, accessed December 12, 2022, https://www.boell.de/en/2016/01/22/ farm-hack-commons-agricultural-innovation.

151. Blythe McVicker Clinchy, "On Critical Thinking and Connected Knowing," Introduction to Service Learning Toolkit, n.d.

152. Claire Nelson, *Smart Futures for a Flourishing World* (Washington D.C.: Changemakers Books, 2021).

153. john a. powell, Stephen Menendian, and Wendy Ake, "Targeted Universalism," Othering & Belonging Institute, accessed October 25, 2022, https://belonging.berkeley.edu/ targeted-universalism.

154. Ibid.

155. James Charlton, *Nothing About Us Without Us*, First (Berkeley, CA: University of California Press, 2000).

156. La Donna Harris and Jacqueline Wasilewski, "Indigeneity, an Alternative Worldview: Four R's (Relationship, Responsibility, Reciprocity, Redistribution) vs. Two P's (Power and Profit). Sharing the Journey towards Conscious Evolution," *Systems Research and Behavioral Science* 21, no.

5 (October 11, 2004): 489–503, https://doi.org/10.1002/sres.631.

157. Ibid.

158. Chris Newman @SylvanaquaFarms "Universal Reciprocity and Mutual Aid, they are not the same and here's why." Instagram. August 18, 2022 https://www.instagram.com/p/ChaagReO-v7/.

159. "THE SKYWOMAN WAY," Skywoman, accessed October 28, 2022, https://www.skywoman.community/the-skywoman-way.

160. Ibid.

161. Rowen White, interview with Emmanuel Vaughn-Lee , Emergence Magazine, podcast audio, October 11, 2019, https://emergencemagazine.org/interview/reseeding-the-food-system/ accessed January 1, 2023.

162. *Elizabeth DeRuff – January 28, 2021,* The Thurman Conversations (Boulder, CO: St. Paul's, Lakewood, 2021), https://www.youtube.com/watch?v=pl3gfggjbP8.

163. "Grain, Bread, Community," *Episcopal News Service* (blog), July 10, 2018, https://www.episcopalnewsservice.org/2018/07/10/grain-bread-community/.

164. Robert Capon, *Supper of the Lamb: A Culinary Reflection* (New York: Farrar, Straus and Giroux, 1989).

165. Vodeb, Oliver. "Food Democracy Critical Lessons in Food, Communication, Design and Art." *Journal of Illustration* 4, no. 2 (2017): 172. *Gale Academic OneFile* (accessed October 25, 2022). https://link.gale.com/apps/doc/A517768412/AONE?u=coloboulder&sid=ebsco&xid=59f7aba4.

166. "The World's 50 Best Restaurants | The List and Awards," UI – 50B – Restaurants – GLOBAL, accessed October 25, 2022, https://www.theworlds50best.com/list/1-50.

167. Eric Weiner, "A Praxis of Pleasure," *3 Quarks Daily* (blog), August 19, 2019, https://3quarksdaily.com/3quarksdaily/2019/08/a-praxis-of-pleasure.html.

168. Michael Moss, "The Extraordinary Science of Addictive Junk Food," *The New York Times*, February 20, 2013, sec. Magazine, https://www.nytimes.com/2013/02/24/magazine/ the-extraordinary-science-of-junk-food.html.

169. Jia Tolentino, "How To Create A Culture Shift." Elle, July 27, 2022 https://www.elle.com/uk/life-and-culture/culture/ a40639030/how-to-create-a-culture-shift-jia-tolentino/.

170. Tema Okun and Kenneth Jones, White Supremacy Culture (2001) https://www.whitesupremacyculture.info/uploads/4/3/5/7/ 43579015/okun_-_white_sup_culture_2020.pdf

171. Melanie Choukas-Bradley, *Connecting with Nature in a Time of Crisis* (Washington D.C.: Changemakers Books, 2020).

172. Anna Lowenhaupt Tsing, *The Mushroom at the End of the World* (Princeton, NJ: Princeton University Press, 2015).

173. Kate Raworth, "Economic Man vs. Humanity: A Puppet Rap Battle | Kate Raworth," September 5, 2018, https:// www.kateraworth.com/2018/09/05/economic-man-vs-humanity-a-puppet-rap-battle/.

174. A. Marshall and Silvia Lozeva, "Questioning the Theory and Practice of Biomimicry," *International Journal of Design & Nature and Ecodynamics* 4, no. 1 (2009), https://www. researchgate.net/publication/235990489_Questioning_the_ theory_and_practice_of_biomimicry.

175. Næss, Arne. "The Deep Ecological Movement: Some Philosophical Aspects". Philosophical Ed. George Sessions. Boston: Shambhala, 1995. 64.

Chapter Five

176. "What I Mean By Postactivism • Writings – Bayo Akomolafe," accessed November 14, 2022, https://www. bayoakomolafe.net/post/what-i-mean-by-postactivism.

177. "Margaret J. Wheatley: Using Emergence to Take Social Innovations to Scale," accessed October 28, 2022, https:// www.margaretwheatley.com/articles/emergence.html.

178. David J. Staley, *Visioinary Histories* (Tempe, AZ: Center for Science and the Imagination, 2022.

179. Sandor Katz, *Fermentation as Metaphor* (White River Junction, VT: Chelsea Green, 2020).

180. "On Slowing Down - Embodiment Matters," accessed November 14, 2022, https://embodimentmatters.com/on-slowing-down/.

181. *Geographies of Racial Capitalism with Ruth Wilson Gilmore – An Antipode Foundation Film*, 2020, https://www.youtube.com/watch?v=2CS627aKrJI.

182. Charles Eisenstein, *The Ascent of Humanity* (2008) available at https://ascentofhumanity.com/text/chapter-4-03/

183. Altieri, M. A. 1995. Agroecology: The Science of Sustainable Agriculture. Boulder, CO: Westview Press.; Gliessman, S. R. 2015. Agroecology: The Ecology of Sustainable Food Systems. 3rd ed. Boca Raton, FL: CRC Press/Taylor & Francis Group.

184. Kimberlé W. Crenshaw, Race, Reform, and Retrenchment: Transformation and Legitimation in Antidiscrimination Law, 101 HARV. L. REV. 1331 (1988). Available at: https://scholarship.law.columbia.edu/faculty_scholarship/2866

185. *Maywa Montenegro de Wit (2021) What grows from a pandemic? Toward an abolitionist agroecology, The Journal of Peasant Studies*, 48:1, 99–136, DOI: 10.1080/03066150.2020.1854741

186. Hakim Bey, *TAZ: The Temporary Autonomous Zone, Ontological Anarchy, Poetic Terrorism*, Second (Autonomedia, 2003).

187. Nicole Civita, "Essential Food System Workers," *Johns Hopkins Berman Institute of Bioethics*, accessed September 27, 2022, https://bioethics.jhu.edu/research-and-outreach/covid-19-bioethics-expert-insights/essential-workers-project/essential-food-system-workers/.

188. Ibid.

189. Alexia Brunet Marks, Nicole Civita, and Hunter Knapp, "Project Protect Food Systems: The Colorado Food Systems

Workers Rapid Response Team Policy Response Agenda," *University of Colorado Law Review*, August 20,2020. https://lawreview.colorado.edu/wp-content/uploads/2020/08/Marks-et-al-Colorado-Coronavirus-CPRA.pdf

190. "Promotora de Salud/Lay Health Worker Program Models – RHIhub Community Health Workers Toolkit," accessed September 28, 2022, https://www.ruralhealthinfo.org/toolkits/community-health-workers/2/layhealth.

191. Ibid.

192. "PROMOTORA NETWORK," PROJECT PROTECT, accessed September 27, 2022, https://www.project protectfoodsystems.org/promotora-network.

193. Ibid.

194. "Agricultural Workers' Rights Bill Explainer (for Distribution).Pdf.Pdf," Google Docs, accessed September 28, 2022, https://drive.google.com/file/d/1B_RSoFfiuodtk8D6_-5nbQ8xnkwSOaJf/view?usp=sharing&usp=embed_facebook.

195. Chappell, M. Jahi. Beginning to End Hunger: Food and the Environment in Belo Horizonte, Brazil, and Beyond. Berkeley: University of California Press, 2018. https://doi-org.colorado.idm.oclc.org/10.1525/9780520966338

196. "What Does It Mean To Be A Queer Business?," Diaspora Co., accessed November 14, 2022, https://www.diasporaco.com/blogs/journal/what-is-a-queer-business.

197. Audre Lorde, *Sister/ Outsider* (Crossing Press, 2007).

198. Lean Logic Dictionary, https://leanlogic.online/glossary/system-scale-rule/

199. Octavia E. Butler, *Parable of the Sower* (New York, NY: Open Road Media, 1993).

200. Alexis Pauline Gumbs, "Alexis Pauline Gumbs | S&F Online | Polyphonic Feminisms," *The Scholar& Feminist Online* 8, no. 3 (Summer 2010): 4.

201. Jason Hickel, *Less Is More: How Degrowth Will Save the World* (Windmill Books, 2021).

202. Bioneers, "john a. powell: Celebrating Diversity to Create an Inclusive Society," *Bioneers* (blog), January 23, 2018, https://bioneers.org/john-powell-celebrating-diversity-create-inclusive-society-ztvz1801/.

203. Ross Gay, *Inciting Joy: Essays* (Chapel Hill, NC: Algonquin Books, 2022).

Note to Readers

Relationality and care do not end on the last page of the book. We want to continue to work together to reset the culture of the food system and the paradigm within which we shape change. For that, we need each other.

Please visit the website for this book at feedingeachotherbook.com and sign up for our mailing list. We won't bug you too much, but we will share anything we think might be of use.

You will also find the complete unabridged version of our citations on the website. If you would like access to all the sources out of which our way of seeing the food system and relationality has developed, you can download a chapter-by-chapter resource compendium for use for your teaching, activism, reading pleasure, or work. We made the choice to slow our scholarly citation roll to make this book readable by anyone and everyone who wants the information. We also are the people who have to stop every page and find all the cited work, and that can get in the way of reading. But, our citation politics matter to us – we want to lift up, honor, and embrace all the researchers, writers, activists, thinkers, and publications we wove together to make this book.

On our website you can also access us. We would love to speak to your class, your book group, your organization, or just to you. So fill out the form and it goes right to our email. This way we can support, cheer you on, or partner as we build our communities of care.

Nicole Civita

Nicole Civita is a human, mother, partner, and friend who is preoccupied with the possible and works like hell to bring its most beautiful bits into being. She's a shapeshifter who has, over the course of her career, taken form as an educator, pracademic, ethicist, attorney, executive, mentor, author, advocate, and consultant. Often, though not always, she's focused her work on shaping change in and through the food system. Nicole's efforts propelled multi-year projects to drastically reduce food waste, revitalize regional food systems, seek justice for agricultural and food workers, explore ethical dilemmas across the food chain, and develop systems-aware, equity-enhancing laws and policies.

Nicole's work is grounded in ecological knowledge, influenced by systems thinking, attentive to relationships of care and reciprocity, and aimed at collective liberation. Through this work, she produces guidance, actionable policy, program, and enterprise recommendations, and truth-telling tools that enable moves toward relationship. She has been nationally recognized for her work on food waste and conservation, harnessing the power of food systems to address the climate crisis, and farmworker justice.

Nicole has learned at least as much from the communities she serves as she did in pursuit of her degrees. She holds an LL.M. in Agricultural and Food Law from the University of Arkansas School of Law, a J.D. from the Georgetown University Law Center, and an A.B. in American Studies and Creative Writing from Columbia University.

In recent years, Nicole has served as Sterling College's Vice President for Strategic Initiatives and the director of its EcoGather initiative and School of the New American Farmstead, as well as faculty and research scholar at the University of Colorado

Boulder, the Johns Hopkins Berman Institute of Bioethics, the University of Arkansas School of Law. Nicole is also a founding co-convener and policy director for Project Protect Food Systems Workers. She is of counsel to Handel Food Law, LLC and also maintains a relational food systems consulting practice: plenty-enough.com

Michelle Auerbach

Michelle is a world-builder and community-maker who uses all her geeky skills to support and educate change shapers. Michelle works as a consultant, educator, and writer focused on change shaping, creativity, and leadership for individuals, organizations, and communities. Michelle has been studying change and developing her change shaping practice for over 40 years. She has worked with institutions (the NY City Department of Health, Kaiser Permanente, and The National Institutes of Health), organizations (from Fortune 50 companies to NGOs and nonprofits) and communities (through activist movements, consulting, designing change processes and facilitating), and she creates communications and storytelling strategies for universities, legislative change groups, and pro-social businesses.

Michelle was trained in facilitation and change management as well as individual and group coaching at the Columbia University School of Public Health, Kaiser Permanente, and the New York City Department of Health as well as through movements and teachers on the ground. She was a professor of Ancient World Languages and Humanities for a decade and served as chair of the Arts and Humanities discipline for the State of Colorado Department of Higher Education. Currently, she teaches communication and story for changemakers at The University of Colorado and Sterling College.

Michelle was also trained as a chef in New York City at the Natural Gourmet, where she studied nutrition, Chinese medicinal cookery. She worked in restaurants and has done food writing for the *New York Times*, the *London Guardian*, and *Sunset Magazine* as well as other outlets. Michelle has a particular passion for supporting food sustainability and justice.

Michelle's PhD dissertation was written on story as a trauma sensitive change technology for individuals, organizations, and communities. She studies the way we respond to change from 6000-year-old wisdom traditions to the neurobiology that drives our connected selves. She is the author of three novels and two books of nonfiction; you can find her at michelleauerbach.com.

CHANGEMAKERS
BOOKS

Transform your life, transform *our* world. Changemakers
Books publishes books for people who seek to become positive,
powerful agents of change. These books inform, inspire, and
provide practical wisdom and skills to empower us to write
the next chapter of humanity's future.
www.changemakers-books.com

The Resilience Series

The Resilience Series is a collaborative effort by the authors
of Changemakers Books in response to the 2020 coronavirus
pandemic. Each concise volume offers expert advice and
practical exercises for mastering specific skills and abilities.
Our intention is that by strengthening your resilience,
you can better survive and even thrive in a time of crisis.
www.resiliencebooks.com

Adapt and Plan for the New Abnormal – in the COVID-19
Coronavirus Pandemic
Gleb Tsipursky

Aging with Vision, Hope and Courage in a Time of Crisis
John C. Robinson

Connecting with Nature in a Time of Crisis
Melanie Choukas-Bradley

Going Within in a Time of Crisis
P. T. Mistlberger

Grow Stronger in a Time of Crisis
Linda Ferguson

Handling Anxiety in a Time of Crisis
George Hoffman

Navigating Loss in a Time of Crisis
Jules De Vitto

The Life-Saving Skill of Story
Michelle Auerbach

Virtual Teams – Holding the Center When You Can't Meet
Face-to-Face
Carlos Valdes-Dapena

Virtually Speaking – Communicating at a Distance
Tim Ward and Teresa Erickson

Current Bestsellers from Changemakers Books

Pro Truth
A Practical Plan for Putting Truth Back into Politics
Gleb Tsipursky and Tim Ward
How can we turn back the tide of post-truth politics, fake
news, and misinformation that is damaging our democracy?
In the lead-up to the 2020 US Presidential Election, *Pro Truth*
provides the answers.

An Antidote to Violence
Evaluating the Evidence
Barry Spivack and Patricia Anne Saunders
It's widely accepted that Transcendental Meditation can create
peace for the individual, but can it create peace in society as a
whole? And if it can, what could possibly be the mechanism?

Finding Solace at Theodore Roosevelt Island
Melanie Choukas-Bradley
A woman seeks solace on an urban island paradise in
Washington D.C. through 2016–17, and the shock of the Trump
election.

the bottom
a theopoetic of the streets
Charles Lattimore Howard
An exploration of homelessness fusing theology, jazz-verse
and intimate storytelling into a challenging, raw and beautiful
tale.

The Soul of Activism
A Spirituality for Social Change
Shmuly Yanklowitz
A unique examination of the power of interfaith spirituality to
fuel the fires of progressive activism.

Future Consciousness
The Path to Purposeful Evolution
Thomas Lombardo
An empowering evolutionary vision of wisdom and the human
mind to guide us in creating a positive future.

Preparing for a World that Doesn't Exist – Yet
Rick Smyre and Neil Richardson
This book is about an emerging Second Enlightenment and the
capacities you will need to achieve success in this new, fast-
evolving world.